# SHOW HER THE MONEY

### THE RIVETING STORIES ABOUT THE PEOPLE BEHIND THE MOVIE AND THE MOVEMENT

CURATED BY CATHERINE GRAY

FOREWORD BY GOLDEN GLOBE & EMMY WINNING ACTRESS SHARON GLESS (CAGNEY & LACEY)

# SHOW HER THE MONEY BOOK ENDORSEMENTS!

"What I love about both the movie and the book, *Show Her The Money,* is how they inspire women and girls to be badass angel investors so we can fund more innovations by women. They demonstrate the importance of women starting funds, investing in venture capital funds, and getting funding from VCs. This can impact the world in tremendously positive ways for generations to come!"

**Rosie O'Donnell**
Comedian, Actress, TV Producer

"*Show Her The Money* honors the trailblazing women of the movie and the movement, who share their stories of resilience and grit in an effort to make the venture landscape more equitable for all."

**Arlan Hamilton**
Founder/Managing Partner, Backstage Capital

"*Show Her The Money* celebrates the fearless and resilient women dedicated to helping other women conquer the last frontier: access to capital. With women investors leading the charge, this book reveals the path forward."

**Alicia Castillo Holley, PhD**
Founder & CEO, Wealthing VC Club, General Partner, Wealthing VC Fund

"The book, *Show Her The Money,* was as riveting and moving as the movie! I highly recommend both!"

**Chealsea Wierbonski**
Group Product Manager, Google, Writer, Keynote Speaker

"By delving into the personal triumphs and challenges faced by women founders and investors, both the movie and the book, *Show Her The Money*, not only entertain but also educate, leaving a lasting impact on its viewers and readers. As the mom of a young daughter and someone who is learning these financial concepts in my 50s, I applaud the contributors of *Show Her The Money* for sharing their stories to elevate the possibilities for future generations."

**Angie Hendrix**
Account Executive, Microsoft

*"Every great dream begins with a dreamer. Always remember, you have within you the strength, the patience, and the passion to reach for the stars to change the world."* - Harriet Tubman

"With *Show Her The Money*, you have a powerful tool, a resource of true stories shared by inspiring, trailblazing, women who have stood in your shoes and navigated the male dominated world of Venture Capitalist to see their dreams realized."

**Susan Anton**
Golden Globe Nominated Actress

"If we all agree that it's unacceptable that only 2% of venture funding goes to female founders, yet women have 52% of the wealth, the solution is obvious: We need more women to invest in venture capital. The movie and this book shine a light on the path. Reading the success stories of other women who have taken this initiative is inspiring, refreshing and hopeful to those interested in manifesting the change we want to see in the world."

**Julie Castro Abrams**
Founder, How Women Invest

# SPECIAL THANKS:

Thank you Toni Purry for your vision, creativity, oversight, and unrelenting dedication. You assembled an amazingly talented team to bring this book to fruition. Thank you Dana LaRue Parks, Enid Flores, Lydia Mack, Jenny Yerrick Martin, Shay Studios, Kim Houser, Cindy Robinson, Mishel Brown and Jentrie Bentley. You are the best for the roles you played in the creation of this book and putting your hearts into this project. It takes a village!

Special thanks to Michaela Kennedy and Roxanne Rodriguez for your dedication to the film tour, book and mission—you are the support system necessary to make it manifest.

And a big shout out and thanks to the extraordinary creators of our movie music! Michele Brourman who did our film's score and who together with Amanda McBroom (who wrote the iconic song, The Rose) created our movie's theme song, *Show Her The Money!*

Very special thanks to Wells Fargo who sponsored our 100 City World Wide Tour, especially through Ruth Jacks, Amy LaBella Rossi, and Judith Goldkrand.

Photo credit: Jentrie Bentley & Shay Studios

Book Cover/Interior Design: Pandalogue Design

# THIS BOOK IS DEDICATED TO:

My wife, Debra Smalley, for her immense and
loving support for my endeavors! You are the absolute best! Love you!

To all the women and men featured in this book
who helped make this film and book a reality!

To my beloved mom, Louise, dad, Donald, and sister, Diana,
who are my angels that are cheering me on, making the impossible possible.

Special shout-out to my niece, Mindy Higgins Bero,
and my nephews, Shane, Chad, and Zach Higgins. You are my heart.

Last but not least, to my lifelong friends who are always cheering me on.
I cherish you: Joanie, Peter, BJ, Di, El, Jack, Julia, Leanne, Jerri G,
Jere B, Mary H, Pat and Sandra.

**With love, Catherine**
**Author, Producer, Lover of Life**

For permission please contact: Contact@showherthemoneymovie.com

Bulk orders can be placed by contacting: Contact@showherthemoneymovie.com

Disclaimer:

The material provided in this book is for general informational purposes only. All content is based on personal experiences, research, and opinions. This book is not intended to replace professional and/or investing advice. The reader should not rely solely on the information provided herein and should seek professional advice or consultation before taking any actions based on the content of this book.

The author does not assume any responsibility or liability for any errors or omissions or for any damages resulting from the use or application of the information contained in this book. All actions taken by the reader based on this information are taken at the reader's own risk.

# TABLE OF CONTENTS

# FOREWORD BY
# SHARON GLESS

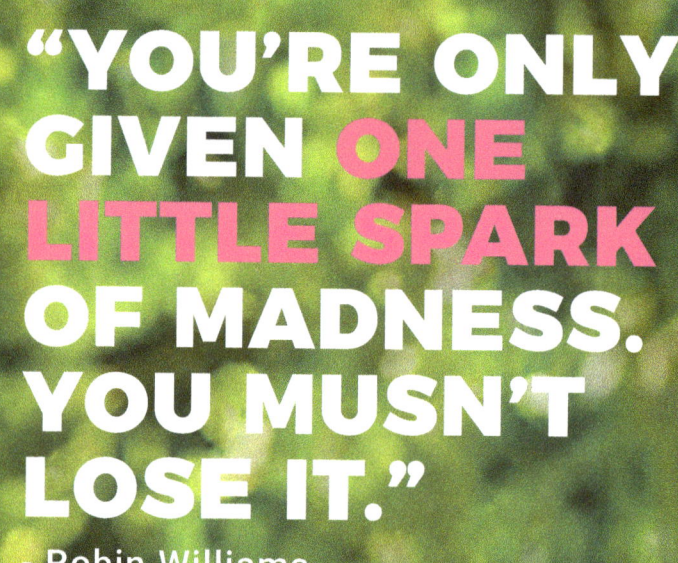

**"YOU'RE ONLY GIVEN ONE LITTLE SPARK OF MADNESS. YOU MUSN'T LOSE IT."**

\- Robin Williams

**SHARON GLESS**
Executive Producer

When my good friend, Dawn Lafreeda, invited me to watch a pitch fest, I had no idea I was about to embark on a journey that would ignite a new passion in me. Standing at the back of that room, leaning against the bar, I found myself swept up in the energy, determination, and vulnerability of women pitching their dreams to other women, women who had the power to make those dreams a reality.

As an actress, I've spent my career bringing characters to life, but nothing could have prepared me for the raw emotion I witnessed that day. One woman in particular, Vicky Pasche from Dapper Boi, touched my heart with her charm and passion, even as she struggled with her presentation. In that moment, I saw a reflection of every actor who's ever forgotten a line on stage but pressed on with determination to get back "on script." It was a powerful reminder that in business, as in acting, our greatest strength is our ability to be vulnerable yet persistent.

The film, *Show Her The Money*, and the book you're holding represent more than just a documentary or a collection of stories. They are a call to action, an invitation to every woman who's ever had a dream but lacked the resources to make it a reality. It's about women helping women, creating a network of support that spans generations and industries.

From my days on *Cagney and Lacey*—the first drama series starring two women on television, watched by tens of millions of people around the world—to today, I have seen the landscape for women change dramatically. Yet, the journey hasn't been without its setbacks. Even with our unprecedented success, *Cagney and Lacey* faced cancellation multiple times, but always the audiences insisted on bringing it back. Women's achievements can be undervalued or dismissed, a problem that persists today in many industries, including business and finance. As I learned through this project, we still have so far to go. But this film and book showcase the incredible opportunity that's unlocked when women invest in women.

When I look at these stories, I don't see just potential for change—I see a reality that is already coming to life. These women aren't just dreaming; they're doing. They're creating, investing, and succeeding against the odds. And in doing so, they're paving the way for countless others to follow.

This message matters now more than ever. As we find ourselves in 2025, it is shocking to realize how little has changed regarding financial equity for women. Despite our progress in many areas, the world of finance and investment remains stubbornly imbalanced. The statistics are sobering: Men still control 98% of venture capital, leaving women with a mere 2%. This disparity isn't just unfair—it's a loss for society as a whole. When women don't get funded, the universe misses out on all the wonderful things women create. Innovation is stifled, potential solutions to global problems go undiscovered, and entire markets remain underserved.

The inequities run deep. It's not just about the lack of funding; it's about the systemic barriers women face at every stage of their entrepreneurial journey. From being taken seriously in pitch meetings to finding mentors who understand their unique challenges, women often find themselves swimming against the current in a system that wasn't designed with them in mind.

But here's the thing: We have the power to change this. This project has shown me that when women come together—when we pool our resources, our knowledge, and our determination—we can move mountains. We can create our own systems, networks, and paths to success.

At its core, this project is about women helping women. It's about recognizing our collective strength and using it to lift each other up. And, while we focus on women empowering women, we hope this movement will inspire more men, like John Majeski and Lorenzo Thione—who you'll read about here—to support women too. Because given the historically stark inequities, it will take all of us working together to create lasting change.

What makes this film and book so powerful is the way they bridge generations. From 30-year-olds starting venture capital funds to 80-year-olds who've been fighting for women's rights for decades, this project showcases the continuity of our struggle and the progress we've made. It reminds us that we stand on the shoulders of those who came before us, and we have a responsibility to pave the way for those who will come after.

Finally, a shout-out to Catherine Gray, the driving force behind this project. Her energy is infectious, her passion palpable. She never stops pitching—not for herself, but for women, for the possibilities, for the future she envisions. It is Catherine's unwavering belief in the power of women supporting women that drew me to this project and keeps me invested in its success.

The stories you'll find in these pages are not just inspiring—they're instructive. They show us what we are capable of when we believe in ourselves and in each other. They provide a roadmap for how we can work together to create change, not just in individual lives but in the very systems that have held us back for so long.

What I hope you take away from this book is the same thing I have taken from being part of this project: a renewed sense of possibility and a call to action. Whether you're a founder with a brilliant idea or a funder looking to make a difference, there is a place for you in this movement. You do not need millions to play this game. One, you just need the willingness to support other women, and two, the courage to take that first step.

As you read these stories, remember that this book is both practical and emotional. It's a "how-to" guide for navigating the world of investment, but it's also a testament to the power of women supporting women. Here is your invitation to join a community that believes in the potential of every woman to change the world.

So come in and play with us. Learn from those who have blazed the trail, and discover how you can be part of this exciting, necessary change. Because when women invest in women, we all win. And

## Connect with Sharon Gless

# EXECUTIVE
# PRODUCERS

# CHAPTER 1

# THE MAKING OF A GLOBAL PHENOMENON

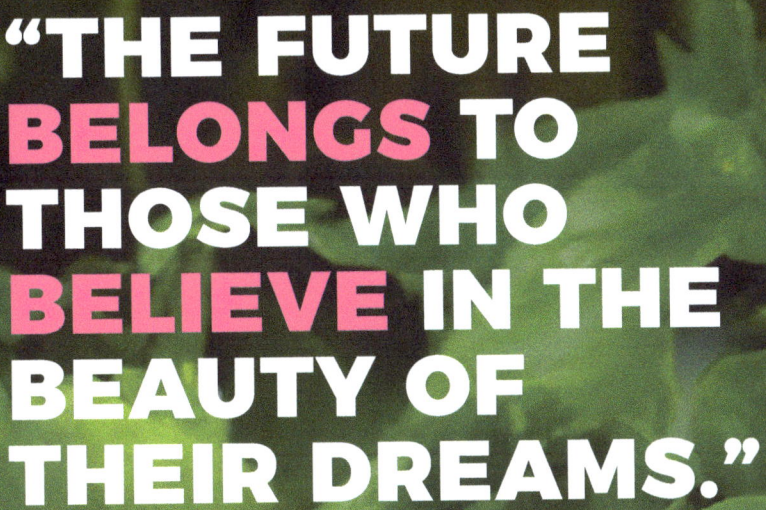

**"THE FUTURE BELONGS TO THOSE WHO BELIEVE IN THE BEAUTY OF THEIR DREAMS."**
- Eleanor Roosevelt

## CATHERINE GRAY
Producer/Executive Producer/Cast

## IGNITING A FINANCIAL REVOLUTION WITH THE MAKING OF A MOVIE

How crazy was it that I was trying to raise money for a movie about how hard it is to raise money!

Now there's an irony—right?!

Encouraged by the challenge, I ended up raising over a million dollars, allowing us to create an award-winning film called *Show Her The Money*. The film not only earned a spot on The Oscar 'For Your Consideration' list and garnered numerous "Best Feature Documentary" awards at festivals across the US, but also sparked a grassroots movement. As a result, my team and I traveled to over 100 cities in the first year to raise awareness and inspire real change.

This book is dedicated to all the remarkable people who made this movie and book possible. Prepare to be deeply inspired by their extraordinary stories, as I was.

## THE BIRTH OF A MOVEMENT

When I first learned that women receive only 2% of venture capital funding while men get 98%, I was astounded. My immediate follow-up question was, "What the heck is venture capital?" And more importantly, "Why are women being so dramatically overlooked?"

As I dug deeper, I discovered that almost everyone I encountered, regardless of their background or success level, had the same reaction. First, they were shocked by the disparity. Then, they admitted that they, too, needed to better understand what venture capital was.

This realization sparked my journey into the world of venture capital, leading to the creation of *Show Her The Money*, the movie and, now, this book. What began as a personal quest for my own understanding has evolved into a mission to educate, inspire, and catalyze change in an industry with far-reaching implications.

My epiphany convinced me: This story had to be told, and it had to be told through film. I've always believed that film and television create awareness and awareness creates change. By presenting venture capital in a heart-centered, storytelling format, we could captivate people and help them understand this complex world in a way that raw data and statistics never could.

So, by creating both a movie and a movement, I decided to coin it a Movie-ment!

## MAKING THE FILM: A COLLABORATIVE EFFORT

Early into my vision for the film, I was at a prestigious Hollywood party. My friend, who was hosting it, introduced me to a well-known Hollywood producer who had just won a Lifetime Achievement Award. She said, "Tell him about your documentary!"

I thought, "Why would this famous producer be interested in my film about women being underfunded in the venture capital world?" Yet, I told him about it. To my surprise, he said, "You know a story that no one else knows and you need to tell that story." I felt so taken aback, yet incredibly validated. When I said goodbye to him on my way out, he reiterated his support! I felt chills, like it was divine intervention—a calling. I knew I had to move forward and raise the money to make it happen.

I imagine that he really doesn't know the impact he had on me, but I was so grateful for that reaffirming message. Many of us never know how we impact other people. As Maya Angelou said, "I've learned that people will forget what you said, people will forget what you did, but people will never forget how you made them feel." That day, he made me feel empowered beyond a shadow of a doubt that I was onto something big, a story that needed to be told.

Central to bringing this vision to life was the extraordinary talent of director Ky Dickens and our incredible editor, Liz Kaar. Ky was my co-producer on this film, and together, we cast an amazing lineup of incredibly smart and fascinating women—fund managers, investors, and entrepreneurs!

Ky always puts her heart into her documentaries and was the ideal director to tell this story. All her films are heart-centered and purpose-driven—she was the perfect partner for this project.

And I can't stress enough the pivotal role that Liz Kaar played as our editor. Liz's exceptional talent for weaving stories together masterfully brought our vision to life. Her ability to find the emotional core of each narrative and connect them into a cohesive, compelling whole was magical. Liz and Ky's contributions were crucial in making *Show Her The Money* not just informative but deeply engaging and emotionally resonant.

The journey of making *Show Her The Money* has been nothing short of transformative. It connected me with extraordinary women (and men!) who invested in the project, believed in its potential, and joined me in promoting the film to ignite a grassroots campaign for change.

# A PERSONAL MISSION

I have always been a believer in living each day as though it were your last because we just never know what might happen.

When my sister, Diana Higgins, unexpectedly passed away at the young age of 69, I reflected on how I wanted to spend my 60s to make an impact with that decade in my own life. I love the saying, "I thought getting old would take longer!" Her passing reminded me of how quickly life goes by and that we never know how long we have on this planet.

I also lost my mom when she was just 74 years old, an age I consider way too young. I was absolutely devastated because I loved her so much. Now that my dad has passed too, I'm the only one left in my immediate family. I wanted to be sure to leave a legacy that would do the Gray name proud.

The other day, a dear friend's daughter, who's like a daughter to me, told me that I inspired her because she felt, at 40, she was already getting old. She said she looked at me and saw that we can still be doing great things later in life, and that it inspired her. I'm so happy to know that I could have this effect on someone younger—and hopefully on many others.

It lights me up to know we are going to create this gender equity in venture capital. Our film is timely with the largest transfer of wealth in history taking place in the coming decade! This is due to the large baby boomer population getting older—many of whom will be leaving their wealth and businesses to their wives and daughters, which is something that happened less in prior decades.

Also, more women than ever are starting their own VC funds too. Now, that's progress.

These women-founded funds are mostly focused on investing in Women, BIPOC, and LGBTQ+ entrepreneurs. Imagine all the brainpower and innovations of these overlooked communities being financed and launched by these funds.

This is a powerful and unstoppable combination to create change!

My wife, Debra Smalley, an amazing writer and real estate broker, has been incredibly supportive of this endeavor. She's helped me raise funds, traveled with me to many screenings, and provided tremendous support as I've toured around the globe! I'm deeply grateful that our visions align—she has been my biggest cheerleader.

## HOW WE CAST THE FILM

Often people ask how the movie was cast.

Originally, a friend of mine, Kathleen Ronald, made a suggestion—that if I was going to make a movie about women in VC, then I had to feature Pocket Sun. I said, Pocket who?

After I met her, I knew she was the right fit. What better superstar to cast than the youngest woman to ever start a venture fund. Of course, it was not easy to reach her.

I emailed her several times, and then one day, I finally got a response. I was over the moon! It was followed by a phone call. I told her I wanted to tell her story in a documentary. She told me a lot of people had said that but never followed through, and I was like, 'Well, I assure you, this film is going to happen. We are going to tell your extraordinary story.'

Once she was onboard, our director Ky and I interviewed the women Pocket had invested in, and based on those interviews—we selected Marian Leitner-Waldman of Archer Roose, Jasmine Jones of Myya and Diipa Büller-Khosla of indē wild—who you will meet in this book.

My first investor in the movie was dynamo, Dawn Lafreeda—whom I knew we needed to feature as an example of a hugely successful businesswoman who was investing in other women. As the female who likely owns the largest number of restaurant franchises in America, Dawn with her movie star looks and fabulous personality was a shoo-in to be cast.

Then I met the brilliant founder of Alternative Wealth Partners, Kelly Ann Winget, at the Wealthy Women Summit organized by Carrie Murray, Founder of The BRA (Business Relationship Alliance) Network. After I suggested that Kelly invest in Dapper Boi, which she did—I knew we had to add that incredible game-changing investment story to the mix.

Plus, it was obvious that the founders, Vicky and Charisse Pasche, who ooze personality and charm, had to be included—and that their incredible journey would make everyone want to cheer them on!

And finally, I knew we had to show other diverse VC women fund founders, so we added the ladies of Emmeline Ventures. This led to adding investor Wendy Ryan—so that women inheriting money like she did, would see themselves in the movie too.

We topped the cast off with trailblazing tech founder H Schuster, who set out to democratize Hollywood. Our goal was for the audience to see themselves in the movie in some capacity—either as a fund manager, who I call the unsung heroes or as an investor or an innovator seeking funding.

# THE GRASSROOTS CAMPAIGN

The funny thing is, when I first declared that we were going to do a 50-city tour, I had no idea how we would make it happen. I remember someone suggesting, "Maybe you should just make it 25 cities?" But I was determined to aim high, saying, "No way, let's shoot for the stars." And what do you know? We didn't just reach the stars—we visited the moon, Jupiter, and Mars, covering over 100 cities and counting!

After our one-week theatrical release in Los Angeles and New York City to qualify for The Oscar 'For Your Consideration' list, the interest started pouring in. Every time we screened the film, we received more requests. The audience's excitement and their social media buzz fueled the explosion of interest, causing the tour to grow and expand organically. Soon, we were getting requests from all over the world. And we continue to get requests!

This was a story that had never been told, and it deeply resonated with women fund managers, investors, potential investors, wealth advisors, family offices, and entrepreneurs across various sectors.

Once the film was completed, we were incredibly fortunate to have the support of Ruth Jacks and Judith Goldkrand at Wells Fargo, who championed our cause. Their backing made it possible for us to take this tour worldwide, turning it into one of the most incredible experiences of my life.

The excitement, joy, and appreciation for the movie and its message have been overwhelmingly exhilarating and rewarding. I call it the "magical mystery tour" because every city's audience generated an enthusiastic energy around the film that felt truly magical. And, in each city, we discovered more brilliant women with game-changing ideas and highly accomplished women ready to invest in shaping the future. Together, we are unpacking the mystery of venture and helping each other build more wealth.

Some of my favorite feedback has been from audience members who say, "I don't usually like documentaries, but this one was so engaging with the storytelling that I loved it." This makes me so happy, as many people think of documentaries as boring. I couldn't be more proud that *Show Her The Money* engages people, and makes them laugh and cry while also educating them about both the simplicity of understanding the venture capital world and emphasizing how important it is to the future of our world.

Throughout this journey, I've had the privilege of connecting with the incredible individuals featured in the film and this book. But it doesn't stop there. These connections have sparked new relationships among these visionaries, creating a powerful network of change-makers. And now, through this book, I'm excited to connect them to you, our readers.

As you dive into these pages, you'll not only learn about the world of venture capital and the inspiring stories of these trailblazers, but you'll also become part of this growing Movie-ment.

My hope is that these stories will inspire you, educate you, and perhaps even motivate you to take action in your own way. Whether you're an aspiring entrepreneur, a potential investor, or simply someone who cares about creating a more equitable world, there's a place for you in this movement.

So, let's embark on this journey together. Let's learn, grow, and work towards a future where innovation knows no gender, where brilliant ideas find the support they need to flourish, and where the benefits of entrepreneurship are accessible to all. Welcome to our Movie-ment!

What's next?

Ultimately- Show Her The Money will be streaming on your favorite networks - watch for it!

## Connect with Catherine Gray

# CHAPTER 2

# CREATING WITH PASSION AND PURPOSE

# "IMAGINATION IS MORE IMPORTANT THAN KNOWLEDGE. KNOWLEDGE IS LIMITED. IMAGINATION CIRCLES THE WORLD."

- Albert Einstein

## KY DICKENS
Director/Executive Producer/Producer

For documentary filmmaker Ky Dickens, the journey to directing *Show Her The Money* was unexpected. Although she had a track record of directing award-winning documentary films that tackle complex social issues, she never imagined immersing herself in the world of venture capital and female founders.

"Ever since I was young, I always had a camera around my neck," she laughs. But her interest in documentary filmmaking began at age 16 when tragedy struck her close-knit friend group, and one of her friends died in a car accident. In the aftermath, Ky found herself with hours of footage she had captured of her friend over the years. Seeing how this visual record helped in the grieving process made Ky realize the power of documenting real life. "It made me realize I only wanted to tell real stories," she reflects. "I wanted to dedicate my life to this thing I love, which is filmmaking, but I wanted to pigeonhole it into telling real stories about people and helping to immortalize that."

Ky's drive to make an impact by making documentary films intensified as she entered adulthood. "I just feel like I always had this very deep sense that I want my life to matter," she reflects.

Each of Ky's films emerged from personal experiences or challenges she was grappling with. Her first documentary, *Fish Out of Water*, was born from her own struggle to reconcile her sexuality with her Christian faith after coming out.

Her next project, *Soul Survivor*, explored the experiences of lone survivors from large plane crashes. This film allowed Ky to work through her own survivor's guilt related to her friend's death years earlier. "That was a really beautiful story about how survivors are victims too; they often carry guilt," she explains.

When Ky became pregnant with her daughter, she confronted the challenges of inadequate parental leave policies in the US—inspiring her third film, *Zero Weeks*, which examined America's lack of paid family medical leave. Through each of these projects, Ky honed her ability to translate personal experiences into universally resonant stories.

Given this pattern, *Show Her The Money* represented a significant departure for Ky. "It was completely out of left field; it didn't reflect my life at all," she admits. When producer Catherine Gray approached her about making a film on venture capital, Ky's initial reaction was uncertainty. "I thought, 'How is that going to be interesting?' because all I understood was a big banking word that didn't apply to my life at all."

But as she delved deeper into the world of female founders and funders, Ky uncovered universal themes that resonated far beyond the realm of venture capital. For example, many of these women struggle with asking for what they deserve, whether in salary negotiations or funding pitches. "I hope this project will help women feel more comfortable valuing themselves and their projects," Ky says.

Approaching the subject as an outsider proved to be an asset. Ky's lack of familiarity with venture capital jargon pushed her to break down complex concepts into simple, relatable terms. "The whole time I was making this film, I was like, 'Is this something that my mother could understand?'" she shares. This focus on accessibility shaped everything from the interview questions to the animations used to illustrate key points.

"I love that these female funders and venture capital managers went out and started funding these women and took matters into their own hands," Ky enthuses, struck by this proactive approach to addressing the funding gap rather than waiting for the existing system to change. These women weren't just writing checks; they were actively working to transform the landscape of entrepreneurship and investment.

Ky also discovered unexpected parallels to her journey as a filmmaker. "Their struggle reflected much of what I've experienced—you have this idea that could change the world, but the funding isn't coming because it's coming from people who don't look like you," she explains. "We too have to make decks, sell ourselves and our vision, often to decision makers that are white, straight men." This realization helped Ky connect more deeply with the subject, allowing her to craft a compelling narrative that resonated far beyond the venture capital world.

Telling the stories of the women in *Show Her The Money* not only changed her perspective on venture capital and investing but also inspired her to take action in a way she never anticipated when she first began the project. By the end of filming, "I ended up becoming so moved, touched, and inspired by what I was seeing that I ended up becoming an investor in a VC fund," Ky shares, still slightly surprised by this turn of events.

For Ky, one of the most rewarding aspects of documentary filmmaking is seeing the real-world impact of her work. With *Show Her The Money*, she's already hearing stories of the film's influence. "I talked to one of the venture capital funds featured in the film and they said every single screening has brought in at least one investor," Ky reports excitedly.

Looking ahead, Ky has big hopes for the film's long-term imprint. "I would love to see, by the time my daughter graduates from college, which is in about ten years, that this has gone from a paltry 2% to, at least, 15-20%," she says, referring to the percentage of venture funding currently going to female founders. "That will feel significant to me."

As both a filmmaker and a mother, Ky sees her body of work as a legacy. "You choose pretty much every line that goes into a movie, every moment, every visual," she reflects. "I hope my kids will watch my work and know exactly who I was, what I cared about, and how I viewed the world."

For aspiring filmmakers and entrepreneurs alike, Ky offers this wisdom: "The only limits to the human mind are those we believe in." This philosophy has guided her own career and is reflected in the determination of the women featured in *Show Her The Money*. By shining a light on their stories, Ky hopes to inspire viewers to push past their own perceived limitations and create positive change in the world.

## Connect with Ky Dickens

# CHAPTER 3

# BUILDING
# A RESTAURANT
# CHAIN EMPIRE

**"YOU ARE THE AVERAGE OF THE 5 PEOPLE YOU SPEND THE MOST TIME WITH."**

- Jim Rohn

# DAWN LAFREEDA

Investor/Executive Producer/Cast

Resilience forged in adversity propelled Dawn Lafreeda from a troubled home to the pinnacle of restaurant ownership and angel investing, shattering glass ceilings and redefining success on her own terms.

Growing up in a tumultuous household, Dawn yearned for autonomy and a better future. "When you come from that kind of a background, where you have no control of your life as a child, you're constantly dreaming of the day that no longer happens to you," Dawn reflects. This early adversity ignited a fierce determination to chart her destiny.

At 23, Dawn seized an opportunity that would change the trajectory of her life—she and a friend purchased her first restaurant, a Denny's franchise, using a combination of credit cards, tips, savings, and a small family loan. "There's a lot to be said about being poor, naive, and young," Dawn muses. "I was worried about taking such a big step, but my mom said, 'What's the worst thing that can happen? You start over at 26.'" "This advice carried me through the many obstacles I would encounter over the years and it would empower me to move past any fear or worry I had."

Eighteen months after her first restaurant purchase, Dawn encountered a significant expansion opportunity stemming from an unexpected source—the oil industry downturn in Texas. This economic shift created a unique situation that Dawn was poised to leverage. She explains, "When oil went bust, Denny's said, 'You know, these stores need an on-site operator. They need love and attention. They need somebody in the market.'"

Seizing this chance for growth, Dawn was offered four stores in West Texas. This proposition marked a pivotal moment in her career, catapulting her from a single-restaurant owner to a multi-unit operator. "So I moved from Orange County, California to West Texas, in Midland-Odessa oil country. I had major culture shock, but again, it was another opportunity," Dawn recalls. While the relocation presented challenges, including adapting to a new environment and navigating the complexities of managing multiple locations, Dawn's flexibility and determination drove her forward.

This expansion not only quadrupled Dawn's restaurant portfolio but also provided valuable experience in operating within volatile local economies tied to specific industries. As her business acumen grew, so did her empire. Dawn bought out her friend's ownership and continued to expand, eventually spreading her operations across seven states. Today, she owns over 75 Denny's restaurants and has owned as many as 117, making her one of the largest multi-unit operators in America and possibly the woman who owns the most restaurants in the country.

But Dawn's success story is not just about building a restaurant empire. It's about breaking barriers and paving the way for other women in business. Throughout her career, she has faced skepticism and bias. "They ask if I inherited [my business], if my husband started it," Dawn says, highlighting the persistent misconceptions about women's capabilities in business.

Despite these challenges, Dawn has remained committed to empowering other women. Her upper leadership team is composed entirely of women, a conscious decision to create opportunities for female professionals in an industry often dominated by men. "Keep fighting the fight," Dawn advises. "Keep empowering women."

Dawn's journey took an exciting turn when she became involved in venture capital and angel investing. Her participation as a judge in the television web series, *Entrepreneur Elevator Pitch*, opened her eyes to the world of startups and the potential for investing in innovative ideas. Being pitched to by so many founders and entrepreneurs, and her memories of struggles to secure funding herself as a young entrepreneur, fueled her passion for supporting other business owners, particularly women.

Learning that women receive only 2% of venture capital funding galvanized Dawn's commitment to change the status quo and inspired her to get involved in *Show Her The Money*. She reflects on the process, "It's really great to be in a room with smart, forward-thinking women. It is exhilarating. And I love it. I love all the women who are involved in the film. They're all special. I mean, they've all done extraordinary things."

Dawn's involvement in *Show Her The Money* has reinforced her commitment to supporting women-led businesses and educating others about the importance of investing in diverse founders. She also hopes the film will inspire more men to invest in women-led companies and encourage women founders to seek out the numerous resources available to them.

As an angel investor, Dawn looks for founders who have their data and business information together and possess a solid track record, rather than those who try to scale too quickly. Dawn's advice to aspiring entrepreneurs and investors is rooted in her own experiences. She emphasizes the importance of asking for help and not being afraid to seek what you need. "More people want to help you than not," she assures. She also advocates for thorough due diligence, encouraging investors to hold founders accountable and to understand the nuances of portfolio management in the startup world.

Dawn suggests exploring franchise opportunities for those interested in becoming business owners, but who still need to figure out where to start. "You don't have to create the idea," she explains. "You want to be a business owner, you want to build an empire, go find a concept that you can learn and build." This approach allows aspiring entrepreneurs to leverage existing systems and relationships while building their own success.

Dawn Lafreeda's story is a testament to the power of perseverance, vision, and paying it forward. She sees her role as an investor as an extension of her lifelong commitment to supporting and empowering others. From her humble beginnings to her current status as a successful restaurateur and angel investor, Dawn continues to break barriers and create opportunities for others. She attributes her success to the support of her life partner Lupita Corbeil and their twin sons, Cruise and Connor. They have  been her biggest cheerleaders  every step of the way and keep her motivated on this journey.

## Connect with Dawn Lafreeda

# CHAPTER 4

# USING YOUR INHERITANCE FOR THE GREATER GOOD

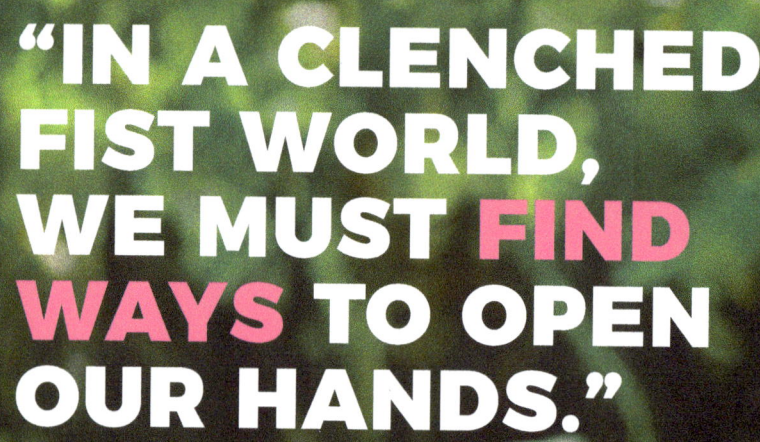

# "IN A CLENCHED FIST WORLD, WE MUST FIND WAYS TO OPEN OUR HANDS."

- Rabbi Dusty Klass

## WENDY RYAN
Investor/Executive Producer/Cast

As an angel investor, author, and leadership development expert, Wendy Ryan is reshaping the venture capital landscape. With a laser focus on supporting women-led businesses and historically excluded entrepreneurs, Wendy's multifaceted journey exemplifies how personal experiences, combined with a keen awareness of privilege, can drive systemic change. Through her innovative approaches to leadership and investing, she opens doors for underrepresented founders and challenges long-standing barriers in the business world.

Her story begins with her founding Kadabra in 2014, a company providing corporate learning solutions for leadership development. This venture was the product of years of experience in the field. "The majority of my career has really been helping leaders find their way, whether that's individually, in teams, or the broader organization," she shares. "What I noticed over many years of doing that work was the very different journey for women than men as leaders."

This observation sparked Wendy's passion for advancing other women's careers. However, the process of starting Kadabra opened her eyes to her own privilege. "At the time I started it, I didn't know what I didn't know," she reflects. "I was able to start a company, be an entrepreneur, and self-fund. I just didn't understand how privileged I was and how few people can do that."

This realization was further amplified by an unexpected transfer of generational wealth following the loss of her parents. The combination of these experiences—recognizing gender disparities in leadership, acknowledging her own privilege, and receiving an unanticipated inheritance—set Wendy on a new path. "I thought, 'What do I have to show for all of this? What will my legacy be?'" Wendy recalls. She began considering how to leverage her position to create a meaningful impact.

Her search for purpose led to two significant endeavors: writing a book and becoming an angel investor. Wendy's book, *Learn Lead Lift: How to Think, Act, and Inspire Your Way to Greatness*, synthesizes her years of experience in leadership development with insights gathered from a diverse array of professionals, from artists to athletes. The book introduces The Learn Lead Lift Framework®, a new leadership model that is inclusive, equity-minded, authentic, and trauma-informed.

Wendy's commitment to equity and inclusion goes beyond writing and investing. In the wake of George Floyd's murder in 2020 and the subsequent racial reckoning, she developed a unique tool to help leaders understand and exercise privilege in a practical, non-threatening way.

"I wondered, how can I help leaders understand the concept of privilege in a way that isn't going to be so triggering?" Wendy explains. Her solution was the creation of The Ryan Privilege Quotient®, a one-page assessment tool anyone can use to determine their General as well as their Situational PQ (Privilege Quotient).

At the heart of Wendy's assessment lies a powerful idea: Privilege functions as a form of social and relational currency, some earned, some inherited. The tool examines nine key categories, including race, gender identity, sexual orientation, and disability. The assessment provides a practical way for people to recognize their own privilege and apply this understanding to their professional environments. For example, Wendy shares, "Picture a meeting you regularly attend. For each form of identity you hold, what percentage of other people at that meeting share the same identity?" Doing this exercise helps people adjust their behavior in productive ways to increase psychological safety, creativity, innovation and ultimately, financial performance.

The goal, Wendy emphasizes, is not to induce guilt but to promote awareness and action. "This is what I love to do—help people get their head around complex concepts like privilege and then, practically, work with this stuff," she says. The positive feedback she's received suggests that her approach is making a difference. "I've heard from people, 'This is the first time I've understood this concept, and now I feel like I can do something with it. Not just feel guilty about it.'"

Simultaneously, Wendy began exploring the world of angel investing with a specific target in mind. "I decided if I'm going to do this, I want to invest in women," she explains. "It scared me. Usually, when something makes me nervous like that, it's a sign that it's something I need to learn or do."

So Wendy joined Golden Seeds, an angel investment group focused on women-led companies. Over the past six years, she has built a diverse portfolio, investing in companies ranging from gender-inclusive clothing brands to Alzheimer's drug research and methane gas recovery systems.

Wendy's goal in angel investing goes beyond financial returns. It's about creating systemic change and opening doors for underrepresented entrepreneurs. "We are democratizing venture capital," she asserts. "We are increasing access to capital for not just women, but for everybody who holds a historically excluded identity."

Wendy's approach to investing is profoundly personal and values-driven. She looks for founders with grit, openness to feedback, and strong communication skills. She's particularly drawn to companies addressing high-leverage problems that can make the world "a better, more interesting, more inclusive, healthier place."

One of her most valuable lessons is the importance of reserving capital for later funding rounds. "The challenges women have don't stop just because they get funding early," Wendy explains. "They're still going to struggle to get Series A, and they're still going to struggle more than men to get Series B."

This realization has shaped Wendy's approach to investing and her advice to other aspiring investors. She emphasizes the importance of understanding portfolio management in this asset class and being prepared to support companies beyond the initial investment.

Reflecting on her journey, Wendy sees her role as an investor as an extension of her lifelong commitment to supporting and empowering others. "My best investments from a psychological, spiritual, emotional perspective are going to be the ones where I look back and say, 'Yeah, that actually changed the game for other female entrepreneurs in a tangible way,'" she shares.

Wendy's commitment to supporting women entrepreneurs is rooted in her understanding of the systemic barriers they face. She cites a startling statistic: "On average, it costs black women $250,000 more to start a company than a white guy." This disparity, often due to limited access to free expertise within their networks, fuels Wendy's passion for investing in companies that can level the playing field.

"If you can't be an investor, don't just sit on the sidelines of this movement or problem," Wendy advises. "You can still do something really impactful." She encourages others to get involved by investing, making intentional purchasing decisions, and using one's network to make introductions and open doors for entrepreneurs.

Wendy's story powerfully reminds us of the potential for individuals to create meaningful change when they combine personal experience with purposeful action.

## Connect with Wendy Ryan

# CHAPTER 5

# FINANCIAL EMPOWERMENT FOR GENERATIONS TO COME

# "THE ONLY THING THAT I KNOW IS I KNOW NOTHING AT ALL."

- Socrates

## DIANA GRESHTCHUK

Investor/Executive Producer

"What is shocking to me is the disempowering beliefs that women have about themselves," says Diana Greshtchuk. Diana is an investor and founder of Fan Your Flame LLC, a financial literacy coaching business that is the direct result of her journey and embodiment of her passion for financial education and empowerment.

The name itself is a clever double entendre, as Diana explains: "Number one, fan your flame, stoke your fire, get even bigger, go brighter. And number two, because I'm a big old homo, I'm like, yes girl, flame!" This playful approach to branding reflects Diana's colorful personality and her desire to make finance more approachable and inclusive. Through Fan Your Flame, Diana offers a range of services designed to demystify the world of finance and investing for women, minorities, and marginalized communities.

Diana's unique perspective of impact investing goes beyond simply writing checks. For her, it's about "investing in another woman, holding the door open so that she can walk through, sit at the table with you, have opportunities to invest and grow, and pass it on."

The seeds of Diana Greshtchuk's journey into finance and investing were planted long before they bloomed. Born in San Jose, California in 1981, she grew up in the heart of Silicon Valley during the dot-com boom. Her father's work at Intel introduced her to the tech world and venture capital from an early age, planting seeds that would later blossom into a multifaceted career in finance, accounting, and investments.

As a child, "I started my own business at six or seven years old, doing lemonade stands and putting flyers in my neighbors' mailboxes about my 'Cinderella Service' to help families with chores," she recalls. Her favorite color was highlighter yellow and she always wanted to be the banker when playing Monopoly—early inclinations that foreshadowed her future path and earned her the nickname "D. Money" in college.

Diana's academic journey led her to major in finance and accounting, eventually becoming a CPA. She spent 12 years at PricewaterhouseCoopers, climbing the ranks to senior manager. Her career path wound through various roles in fund accounting, auditing, and financial management, providing her with a comprehensive understanding of the investment world's inner workings.

But in May 2020, Diana's world was rocked when she lost her mother only seven years after her father passed away, leading to what Diana calls her "dark night of the soul". As an only child, she received a small inheritance and found herself at a crossroads. "I was sitting there asking myself, 'What is my legacy? What am I doing here?'" she reflects.

Diana hired a life coach for support, who opened her life to a transformative new perspective. "I invested in myself first by just starting to see what would make me happy, because my mother wanted me to be happy. When you look at what's important to you, your definition of success, you know, how many hours of the day are you spending in the emotions that you want to feel? How do you want to feel each day? So for me, it really became about alignment and spending as much time as possible in gratitude, passion, and limitlessness."

She found the experience so powerful that she was inspired to pursue a coaching certification herself, adding another dimension to her already diverse skill set. "I thought about legacy and the things that I believe in," Diana explains. This realization led her to focus on impact investing, particularly in female entrepreneurs. "I think overall, they're way underestimated out there," she notes.

This philosophy is evident in her involvement as an investor and executive producer for *Show Her The Money*. Diana sees the film as a way to make finance accessible for people who don't yet speak the language of finance. "I want little girls to watch it. I want little nonbinary BIPOC and LGBTQ youth watching it," she says, emphasizing her desire to start financial education early and make it accessible to as many groups as possible.

She developed an "Investing 101" course specifically for those inspired by *Show Her The Money*, walking people through the basics of what they need to know to get started. Looking to the future, Diana is excited about the potential impact of *Show Her The Money* and her ongoing work with Fan Your Flame. She envisions a world where financial literacy is taught from a young age, where diverse founders have equal access to capital, and where impact investing becomes the norm rather than the exception.

Diana's advice for aspiring investors reflects her holistic approach to finance. For those who feel they don't have the means to invest, she recommends starting with a "money date"—an honest assessment of one's financial situation. "Get financially literate and figure out where you are because that's your Point A," she advises. From there, she encourages people to start small, even if it's just buying partial shares or setting aside a portion of a tax refund.

For those who have the means but lack the knowledge, Diana suggests, "Talk to a network of like-minded people who also want to invest but are still learning. Talk to a financial coach." She also emphasizes the importance of addressing any disempowering beliefs that might be holding you back.

Diana's investment approach is not just about financial returns. "I want to see that the company is going to make a positive difference in the world," she states. This could mean job growth in a region, healthcare innovations that save lives, or companies that challenge, disrupt, and expand societal norms.

Through her investments, educational programs, and advocacy work, Diana's committed to fanning the flames of financial empowerment for generations to come and she continues to balance her roles in the institutional private equity fund space, as an impact investor and financial educator.

## Connect with Diana Greshtchuk

# ASSOCIATE PRODUCERS/ INVESTORS

# IN 2024, WOMEN OWNED 14.5 MILLION BUSINESSES, WHICH IS 39.2% OF ALL EMPLOYER FIRMS.

Source: Wells Fargo "Impact of Women-Owned Businesses Report"

# CHAPTER 6

# BREAKING BARRIERS IN VENTURE CAPITAL FUNDING

"IF THEY TELL YOU YOU CAN'T DO SOMETHING, **IT'S BECAUSE THEY CAN'T.** THEY DON'T KNOW WHAT YOU ARE CAPABLE OF."

- Pocket Sun

## POCKET SUN

Investor/Associate Producer/Cast

Amidst the polished boardrooms and sleek pitch decks of the venture capital world, a revolution is brewing. At its helm stands Pocket Sun, a force of nature who's rewriting the rules of the game.

In the Northern Chinese province that gave rise to Confucius, Pocket navigated a childhood steeped in rigid patriarchal traditions. Yet, even as a child, she exhibited an insatiable curiosity and a penchant for performance. "I was an extrovert," Pocket recalls. "I was eager to learn. I was a very early reader. I love to say I was always kind of performing in front of people."

Her parents' sacrifices nurtured this early confidence. "My parents didn't have any educational opportunities so they really invested in mine," she recalls. "I grew up becoming a pianist. And my dream when I was in elementary school was to become a music producer. When I was in second grade, they were making a few hundred RMB a month," Pocket shares. And yet, somehow, magically, they saved enough money to buy me a piano, which cost like 8600 RMB." This early investment in her future would shape Pocket's understanding of the power of strategic support.

Early on, Pocket cultivated a budding entrepreneurial spirit. In middle school, she became fascinated with her first pop star idol and took to the streets, making flyers and advocating for votes for them to win a competition. This early experience in championing what she believed in would later inform her approach to venture capital.

Pocket's journey took a significant turn when she became the first in her family to attend college, venturing far from home to The College of William & Mary in Virginia. The cultural shift was seismic. "I couldn't understand people's humor. I couldn't understand the cultural references, and I couldn't make great conversations," she shares. This experience of feeling like an outsider would later fuel her passion for supporting underrepresented entrepreneurs.

The genesis of SoGal came during Pocket's time at the University of Southern California while pursuing her master's degree in entrepreneurship and innovation. "I couldn't help but fall in love with the world of entrepreneurship and startups in business, but quickly realized that I was always one of the only women and Asians in the room. I didn't feel like I belonged anywhere in the startup space. And that's what drove me to start the community first," she recalls. "And through that, we realized that all these women needed funding, but no one was providing it. So, it became the huge, universal bottleneck I had to help solve as an entrepreneur. And that's how I realized that being in venture capital and becoming the funding source was the only way to go if I were to solve the real problem."

What began as a student organization quickly blossomed into something much more significant. Despite skepticism from professors and peers, Pocket's inaugural SoGal Summit drew nearly 500 attendees, signaling an unmet need in the entrepreneurial community. "No one thought I could pull it off," Pocket remembers. "I got a lot of rejections, even from my own professors."

A May 2015 Stanford program on venture capital radically altered Pocket's path. There, she met her future co-founder, Elizabeth Galbut, and had a revelation: "If we can't find the VC firm that we want to work for, we just have to start our own." This audacious idea, born from a sense of exclusion and a desire for change, would become SoGal Ventures.

Launching a venture capital fund at 24 was no small feat. Beyond the typical entrepreneurial hurdles, Pocket grappled with the immense responsibility of stewarding other people's investments. "It's pretty astronomical amounts of money that we're dealing with as 24-year-olds," she reflects. "I had a lot of insecurity and kind of this mindset of, 'What if I fuck up? What if I don't do a good job? What if I ruin relationships? What if I ruin someone's retirement?'"

To navigate these challenges, Pocket and her co-founder embarked on a journey of self-discovery and personal growth. They worked with coaches and therapists, delving deep into their psyches to understand and overcome their limiting beliefs. This internal work became a cornerstone of their approach to investing and mentoring founders.

SoGal Ventures emerged with a clear mission: to invest in "undervalued founders, undercapitalized geographies, and underserved problems." Pocket's vision extends beyond mere profit-making. "We are idealistically building almost an art gallery of what we think the future should look like," she explains.

Pocket tempers her idealism with a pragmatic approach to identifying promising founders. She looks for visionaries who are resourceful, adaptable, and deeply connected to the problems they're solving. "I love hearing people talk about, 'This is where I think the future should be. And this is how we could change the world in the next decade,'" she says.

Pocket envisioned SoGal Ventures as a disruptive force in VC that would shine a spotlight on the brilliant ideas lurking in the industry's blind spots. Pocket notes, "We love mission-driven founders. We love people who can do a lot with a little. We're looking for people who are challenging the status quo the way we challenged the status quo when we started SoGal."

Despite the obstacles and slow progress in changing industry demographics, Pocket remains optimistic, finding motivation in the individual stories of the entrepreneurs she supports. "Each of them, you know, has their own hero's journey, and it's not linear. You get to be a part of that," she reflects.

Pocket views the enduring funding disparity for women entrepreneurs as a rallying cry for change in the industry. "It's been super slow to change," Pocket admits. "I've been in this business for almost 10 years now, and still, women only get 2%."

Pocket's approach to investing is extremely personal and purpose-driven. She encourages women to view investing as an extension of their personality and interests. "Investing is also a way of getting access to things, getting access to different networks, different opportunities and possibilities in your life," she explains.

For women interested in investing, Pocket offers: "Really have a hell of a vision, like imagine your dream life. Think big." She emphasizes the importance of long-term thinking and aligning investments with personal values. "I think investing is so much fun," she adds, encouraging women to explore different investment vehicles and keep an open mind.

Looking to the future, Pocket envisions SoGal as a platform for seeding ventures across various industries, from healthcare to media. "We really want to build a big enough, good enough platform so that others want to jump on board and lead those ships alongside us," she says.

This expansive vision includes the idea of a SoGal hospital, insurance company, publishing house, and film production company. "Because all of these spaces were not for us, by us, right?" Pocket explains. "So how do we cultivate new talent, new storytellers, new voices, new faces, to be on the forefront?"

The impact of SoGal's work is tangible. With about $50 million under management and a portfolio of 46 companies, Pocket and her team are actively reshaping the entrepreneurial landscape. Each investment represents not just a financial commitment, but a vote of confidence in a more diverse and inclusive future of business.

Pocket's journey is far from over. She continues to learn and grow, facing each new challenge with the same determination that led her to start SoGal. "You're only as good as your latest deal, no matter what you know you have achieved in the past," she reflects, embracing the constant evolution required in the world of venture capital.

With each investment, Pocket Sun redefines venture capital, proving that courage and conviction can reshape an entire industry. "The SoGal spirit and ethos are very transferable in other spaces," she asserts. Pocket's journey shows that true change comes from those bold enough to envision and build a different future.

## Connect with Pocket Sun

# CHAPTER 7

## CHANGING THE FACE OF VENTURE CAPITAL

# "IT ALWAYS SEEMS IMPOSSIBLE UNTIL IT'S DONE."

- Nelson Mandela

## BRIDGETTE L. SMITH

Investor/Associate Producer

Bridgette L. Smith's ascent in the venture capital world reads like a masterclass in curiosity, resilience, and the art of paying it forward. "I'm in alignment with my higher purpose," she declares, her voice resonating with conviction. "I am here to support and fund women, people of color, and founders who are LGBTQ."

But the path that led her to this mission was anything but a straight line—it was a winding road paved with unexpected turns and moments of divine intervention. Bridgette's career began in television, both in front of and behind the camera. She was a news reporter, talk show host, and even a campaign spokesperson for a mayoral candidate. Her expertise in media extended to print journalism and public relations, giving her a comprehensive understanding of communication across various platforms.

However, the volatility of the media industry led Bridgette to seek additional income streams. "There are ebbs and flows in the media world," she explains. This search for stability led to an unexpected turning point when she stumbled upon a job listing for a technical writer.

"I thought it was going to be a part-time job to pay some little bills on the side," Bridgette recalls. Little did she know that this seemingly insignificant decision would open up an entirely new set of opportunities. "As God would have it, it opened up a whole new world of technology for me."

Embracing her natural curiosity, Bridgette dove headfirst into the tech industry. She taught herself programming languages, downloaded free manuals, and watched countless YouTube tutorials. Her dedication paid off as she steadily climbed the corporate ladder, transitioning from technical writer to business analyst, project manager, program manager, and eventually to the C-suite.

However, reaching the top came with its own barriers. "It was a very lonely place. Isolating. I was the only woman, the only person of color," Bridgette admits. "I had one sponsor who was with me every step of the way—always pushing the envelope and pushing me into rooms and getting people to listen to me. But it was so exhausting to constantly be at battle with white men who didn't see me as an equal. I had earned my way into the room." Despite these obstacles, she persevered, leveraging her communication skills and newfound technical expertise to excel in her role.

As Bridgette became more weary over the weight of her position, "Google came along at the right moment and swept me off my feet," she recalls, and offered her a chance to join their executive team. The process was rigorous, involving 14 interviews over the span of a year. "I said, let me see what this is about because this is such a magnificent opportunity. I did not want to pass it up. And so I took my time with it. I took every call; I explored every possibility," she says.

The move to Google brought with it a relocation to Silicon Valley from Milwaukee, Wisconsin, introducing Bridgette to an entirely new environment. "I'm a Midwest girl," she explains. "I'd never lived in Silicon Valley. I'd never lived anywhere other than Wisconsin." This cultural shift, combined with her experiences at Google, exposed her to the world of venture capital, unicorns, and private equity—concepts entirely foreign to her then.

At Google, Bridgette encountered her next pivotal moment. She often heard her male colleagues discussing their investments and returns in pre-meeting conversations. "They were talking in code," she remembers. "I did not have a clue what they were talking about." Rather than feeling discouraged, Bridgette rose to the occasion. "Anytime you challenge a person like me, and you try to marginalize and minimize, all you're doing is activating me."

Emboldened by these new ideas, Bridgette began to educate herself about investing. She researched, studied, and slowly began to put her toe in the water. Her first investment was a modest $2,500 through an online portal. "I wanted to undo or hit the refund button almost instantly," she laughs, recalling her initial nervousness.

But Bridgette didn't stop there. She continued to learn, taking meticulous notes during investor calls. "I started to catalog every single question that was go-to-market specific, product specific, founder specific, sector-specific, terms specific, and exit specific," she explains. This diligence paid off, and soon, Bridgette could assess potential investments quickly and effectively.

As her confidence grew, so did her portfolio. From 2021 to 2024, Bridgette went from having no investments to a portfolio of 264 companies, including direct investments, special purpose vehicles, and venture capital funds. "I now teach women how to invest," she says proudly. "At last count, I've taught over 6,000."

At the heart of Bridgette's investing philosophy lies a profound commitment to supporting specific groups. As she clearly states, "I am here to support, to fund women, people of color, and founders who are LGBTQ. That is my scope." Her investment choices reflect this mission, focusing on entrepreneurs with historically less access to venture capital funding.

Her commitment to this cause extends beyond just writing checks. Bridgette holds open office-hours three days a week, offering 15-minute slots for anyone who wants to pitch her, ask questions, or seek advice. "It only takes me 15 minutes to help somebody," she says. This generosity has led to unexpected connections and opportunities, with high-profile individuals often appearing on her public calendar.

Bridgette sees even more possibilities as she looks to the future. She's working on obtaining various licenses, including her Series 65 and Series 63, which will allow her to become a broker-dealer. "Once I finish my licenses...the whole scenario becomes even wider," she explains excitedly.

Bridgette has remained grounded in her faith and desire to help others throughout her life. "I am blessing people. I am spreading God's word. I am doing his work," she says. This sense of purpose has guided her through each phase of her career, from television to tech and now to venture capital.

As she continues to break barriers and open doors for others, Bridgette Smith is not just changing the face of venture capital—she's redefining what's possible for women, people of color, and LGBTQ individuals in business and beyond.

### Connect with Bridgette L. Smith

# CHAPTER 8

## INVESTING INTENTIONALLY

**"WHEN A DOOR IS HARD TO OPEN, AND IF NOTHING ELSE WORKS, SOMETIMES YOU JUST HAVE TO REAR BACK AND KICK IT OPEN."**

- Muriel Siebert

**KELLY ANN WINGET**

Investor/Associate Producer/Supporting Cast

At just 15 years old, Kelly Ann Winget stood behind the counter of a car wash dreaming of expensive jeans. Little did she know, this job would ignite her entrepreneurial spirit and set her on a path to disrupt the venture capital and private equity world.

"I started upselling all the customers at the register when they would check out," Kelly recalls. Her natural talent for sales quickly became apparent, forcing the company to adjust its commission structure repeatedly to keep up with her stellar performance. Kelly's ingenuity and drive foreshadowed a career defined by unconventional thinking and a relentless pursuit of opportunity.

The following years saw Kelly juggling multiple jobs, each adding a new dimension to her growing business savvy. By her early twenties, she managed 16 locations for a group of radiologists—a role that exposed her to diverse business models and personalities. This eclectic experience would later prove invaluable, informing her unique investing approach and shaping her wealth management perspective.

A watershed moment came while Kelly was working at a demolition company. For months, she sat alongside a consultant, together developing a cost-estimating software. Despite doing most of the work herself, Kelly watched as the consultant walked away with a $60,000 check for what she saw as minimal effort.

Frustrated but undeterred, Kelly approached the company owners. "I want the salary. This is the work that I did," she asserted. When they balked, Kelly made a bold decision. "I'm going to become a business consultant and make six figures," she declared, armed with a new mantra: "If he can do it, so can I."

With characteristic determination, Kelly transformed her career. Within four months, she landed a six-figure business consulting role in Newport Beach, California, proving her capabilities and setting the stage for her future in disruptive investing.

From there, Kelly's path wound through various roles in investor relations, family office, and private wealth management. Each position added another layer to her growing expertise, culminating in a bold move in 2020. Drawing on her abundance of experience and driven by her innovative vision, Kelly founded Alternative Wealth Partners, a private equity company designed to challenge traditional investment models.

"I didn't see a product out there that leveraged all the incentives across different asset classes in a singular investment," Kelly explains. Her progressive approach aims to provide retail investors access to diversified alternative investments typically reserved for ultra-high-net-worth individuals and family offices.

What sets Kelly's funds apart is their diversity and tax advantages. Her first fund included 28 portfolio companies across various sectors, from oil and gas to fintech. By creatively leveraging tax incentives and using losses from one sector to offset gains in another, she maximizes returns for investors.

Kelly's approach goes beyond mere financial engineering. She is driven to invest in and rebalance the business world. "I want to invest in historically white, male-dominated industries and turn them into women-owned businesses," she asserts. This philosophy led her to acquire an ammunition company, making it the only woman-owned primer manufacturer in the world.

Her investment strategy often prioritizes long-term progress over quick exits. "I try to build incentive programs that motivate the founder to stay in their business and grow it sustainably," she explains. This approach includes milestone clauses that allow founders to buy back equity as they hit specific targets.

Focusing on "generational businesses"—companies that can last for 100 years or more—Kelly is particularly interested in energy, infrastructure, and manufacturing, sectors often overlooked by traditional venture capital.

Challenging industry norms, Kelly revolutionized how she interacts with married investors. She observed how wives were often sidelined in financial discussions and instituted a new rule. "When I started my own firm, I made sure both people were in the room if it was a husband and wife," she explains. This inclusive strategy has proven successful, often resulting in investments from both spouses.

She has also significantly diversified her investor base. "Even in my oil and gas fund, almost 70% of investors are women or people of color," Kelly notes. "If I can make a black woman wealthier, then I've helped solve the problem."

However, Kelly doesn't discriminate against any potential investors. "All money is green," she quips, noting that she's happy to take investments from "rich white dudes" alongside her more diverse investor base. She sees this as redirecting capital toward underrepresented founders and industries.

"It's important for investors to realize that you don't have to support in the way you think, like, by just giving money," she explains. "It's about understanding where somebody is and providing the right kind of support." This perspective informs Kelly's current approach to growing businesses in her investment portfolio.

Along the way, Kelly has learned hard lessons about investor alignment and managing expectations. "Getting large checks from impatient people is probably the hardest lesson everyone will learn," she reflects.

Despite these hurdles, optimism about the future of investing and the role of women in finance permeates Kelly's outlook. She notes that women often make excellent investors in venture capital and private equity due to their patience and commitment once they've made a decision.

Looking back, Kelly wishes she had started her firm earlier. Her advice to aspiring entrepreneurs? "When you get the feeling in your gut, just do it," especially when others encourage you to leap.

As trillions of dollars are set to change hands in the coming years, Kelly sees an opportunity for women to step into more active investing roles rather than focusing solely on philanthropy. "It's not our responsibility to save the world by giving away our wealth," she argues. "We can actually have more impact by being intentional investors."

Through her innovative approach to investing, commitment to diversity, and willingness to challenge industry norms, Kelly is not just participating in the investment world—she's actively reshaping it. Her story is an inspiration and a roadmap for those looking to disrupt the status quo and create more inclusive financial ecosystems.

### Connect with Kelly Ann Winget

# CHAPTER 9

## DEFYING
## THE ODDS

# "NEVER, EVER BE AFRAID TO MAKE SOME NOISE AND GET IN GOOD TROUBLE, NECESSARY TROUBLE."

- Congressman John Lewis

## SILVIA MAH

Investor/Associate Producer

As a scientist-turned-investor with a PhD in biochemistry and molecular biology, Silvia Mah brings a distinctive perspective to venture capital. Her journey to becoming an advocate for women in entrepreneurship is as diverse as the founders she supports, shaped by an upbringing that defied conventional boundaries.

Born in Caracas, Venezuela, Silvia's early life was a study in cultural diversity and adaptability. Her father, an orphan from WWII Italy, survived a firing squad and a political prison in Nazi Germany, and eventually became a successful entrepreneur in Venezuela. Her mother, a Stanford graduate, conducted military analysis of WWII Europe for the CIA before being deployed to Venezuela to continue the work. This unique family background set the stage for Silvia's own journey, instilling in her values of resilience, adaptability, and seizing opportunities.

For many years, Silvia's primary focus was on science. Driven by a passion for understanding the world around her, she pursued a PhD in biochemistry and molecular biology at Scripps Institution of Oceanography. Her academic journey, however, was far from typical, as Silvia navigated the complex world of balancing rigorous academic pursuits with the demands of motherhood and caregiving. "I had two children during my PhD, which is not a great idea," Silvia admits with a hint of wry humor. When her second child was born with special needs, requiring frequent hospital visits and the use of a wheelchair, she decided to stay in San Diego.

Silvia's path took an unexpected turn when "A deep sea sediment professor had some funding from NASA. And he said, 'Do you want to work with me for a year on this crazy project that I have?'" Silvia recalls. "I'm like, sure, that means staying here, using my PhD for something. I can't go the academic route because I have to take care of my son with cerebral palsy, but I'll do this." Her acceptance of his offer marked the beginning of her transition from pure science to the world of innovation and entrepreneurship, which led to further positions, including working at the engineering school at UCSD, where she continued to notice a glaring gender disparity in STEM fields.

This observation became a driving force in Silvia's career. She pursued an MBA to gain more business acumen, initially intending to start her own company or merge science and business in the booming biotech industry in San Diego. During her studies, she continued her efforts to support women in business, creating various women's organizations and programs within the MBA community. However, as Silvia was nearing the completion of her MBA, a pivotal moment arrived when her father passed away, leaving her with an unexpected inheritance.

The inheritance jolted Silvia into a new perspective, crystallizing the complex family dynamic that had shaped her view of women's roles throughout her life. "My whole life, my father thought I could only be his secretary," Silvia explains. "That's all he thought I could amount to as a woman, even though my mother was super-educated." This limiting view stemmed from her father's background, while her mother provided a powerful counterbalance as a strong feminist.

Motivated by this dichotomy, Silvia made a decisive choice. "I'm going to work until the day I die because I'm a workhorse, but I can actually activate my capital for good. And in his honor, I only invest in women-led businesses." This decision in 2010 marked the beginning of Silvia's journey as an angel investor focused on supporting women entrepreneurs.

Silvia quickly realized that to make a significant impact, she needed to do more than just write checks. "My check is kind of small," she admits. But how I can amplify my dollars is through network, resources, and mentorship. I can give founders the financial capital, but I can also give them the relational capital and the resource capital to thrive."

This holistic approach to investing has become Silvia's signature. She is the Chairwoman & Founder of Stella Foundation, a national conSTELLAtion of organizations and leaders walking alongside women-led businesses from startup to sale, and the funders who champion them. The foundation's signature programs include Stella Labs, an accelerator for female entrepreneurs to launch and scale, Women's Venture Summit; and an angel group for women investors called Stella Angels. She's also the General Partner of Stella Impact Capital and Partner at Ad Astra Ventures alongside 2 other partners where resilient female founders receive conscious capital.

With a clear investment thesis, Silvia invests in diverse women founders at the pre-seed and seed stages, typically writing checks between $5,000 and $25,000. She actively supports these early-stage companies, often taking a board seat and helping throughout the startup's journey.

Among Silvia's standout investments is Uqora, a UTI-prevention drink mix company. "I love her journey," Silvia says of the founder. "She started with a pitch competition that we ran at Stella Foundation. We supported her pitch prep, and she won our local competition and then a national competition, gaining $75K from the Sara Blakely Foundation. About a year and a half later, she opened up a round for angels like me." Uqora eventually exited to Pharmavite, the company behind Nature Made® vitamins, providing Silvia with a significant return that she primarily reinvested in her foundation to continue supporting women entrepreneurs.

Another success story is Aquacycl, a deep tech company in water purification. The founder came to Stella as a postdoctoral with limited business knowledge. "She told me, 'I don't know how to do a financial projections spreadsheet,'" Silvia recalls. "And we walked her through it. There was no shame. We just dove in and connected her to the right people." Today, Aquacycl provides water purification solutions for major corporations like Pepsi, Anheuser-Busch, and Mars Candy.

While these success stories fuel Silvia's passion, she's also candid about the challenges. "The toughest lesson is the long haul," she admits. "I knew from the beginning that it would be five to seven years of waiting for return on investment. But when it's all cumulative, when you have 160 companies, spanning many industries for the upside of portfolio theory, and you don't have the capital that you can use daily, it gets a little squirrely."

Despite these challenges, Silvia remains committed to her mission. She draws inspiration from figures like Congressman John Lewis, whose famous quote, "Get into good trouble, necessary trouble," has guided her through difficult decisions in her career when progress is a must but it necessitates change and advocacy that makes people unhappy or upset.

Looking to the future, Silvia focuses on moving the needle for women in venture capital. "I dare to dream of a different world," she says. "I dare to dream of women getting to even 50% representation across the venture table, across the angel investor table, and entrepreneurs getting funded."

As she continues investing, mentoring, and advocating for women entrepreneurs, Silvia Mah stands as a beacon of change in the venture capital world. Working to reshape the landscape, Silvia is not just investing in women founders—she's investing in a more equitable future for all entrepreneurs.

## Connect with Silvia Mah

# CHAPTER 10

# MAKING HISTORY-INVESTING IN WOMEN

**"STEP OUT OF THE HISTORY THAT IS HOLDING YOU BACK. STEP INTO THE NEW STORY YOU ARE WILLING TO CREATE."**

- Oprah Winfrey

# JOHN MAJESKI

Investor/Associate Producer

In the heart of Silicon Valley, where innovation and disruption are the norm, John Majeski is embarking on a mission that's both revolutionary and long overdue. As a seasoned entrepreneur and investor with exits and large scale integrations to and with tech giants like HP, Dell, and Lenovo, John is now turning his attention to what he sees as one of the biggest missed opportunities in venture capital: investing in women founders.

John's journey to becoming an advocate for women in entrepreneurship was multifaceted. Growing up, he was always curious and entrepreneurial, taking things apart to understand how they worked. But his home life profoundly shaped his perspective on the challenges women face in the business world.

His childhood seemed typical of a middle-class household, but the impacts of its hidden struggles only became clear with time. "My father was a functional alcoholic," John explains. "He was very gainfully employed but the drinking obviously changed his personality. It's not like he got violent, but he was drunk and it was very discouraging, especially those times where I would have liked to have his help with homework or life in general. In hindsight, it's even more powerful than it was actually experiencing it. As a kid, you sort of accept it and figure out how to get by and work with those windows of non-drinking time."

John's admiration for his mother deepened as he learned about the challenges she faced in her pursuit of education and career. "She has a unique Italian-Argentinian last name," John shares. "When she applied to a prominent university, they probably thought it was a guy. When she met with the school, she was told that the engineering program was only for men, as engineering is 'a man's job.'" This wasn't an isolated incident. John's mother faced similar rejections from other opportunities, consistently being steered away from engineering and towards teaching instead, even though early in her career she worked as a "draftsman" for GE, producing technical drawings. Fortunately, she fell in love with teaching and even went on to get graduate degrees in education.

Reflecting on his mother's resilience, John continues, "I'm just thinking about what my mother had to do to keep the family together as a very busy public school teacher—grading homework at night, developing lesson plans, trying to make the best of an at-times challenging relationship. John had wondered  if she would have moved on if she were assured of financial wellbeing and if divorce weren't as taboo as it was in the '70s.

Without knowing it at the time, observing his mother's resilience at home and learning about the obstacles she encountered in her education and career laid the foundation for John's future advocacy for women in business.

John's perspective further evolved when he became a single father. After a divorce, he and his young daughter relocated to Silicon Valley for his tech career. Raising a child in the tech industry's epicenter provided John with a front-row seat to the systemic challenges women face in this field.

"As my daughter progressed through school here, I became acutely aware of the persistent issues affecting women and the reasons behind their marginalization," John reflects. "It hit me then: This situation desperately needs to change."

This realization, coupled with the lessons from his childhood, galvanized John's commitment to championing gender equality in the business world, particularly in the male-dominated realm of venture capital, and soon led to a pivotal moment in his career.

John's involvement with *Show Her The Money* began through a serendipitous connection. "There's a woman I've known in venture capital for years in Silicon Valley," John explains. "She said, 'I know that you have an affinity for investing in women and underrepresented founders. You need to meet my friend, Catherine, who's making a movie.'"

Upon meeting Catherine and learning about the film, John was immediately captivated. "I thought, oh my gosh, this is huge, I'm in. And I didn't know the statistics were as bad as they were."

This introduction proved to be the ultimate catalyst for John's newest venture, a fund focused on women entrepreneurs. While trying to drum up support for the film among his fellow male VCs, he was shocked by their reactions. "I was shocked when I talked to some of my male VC brethren," John says. "Let's just say it was challenging to get support for the movie."

The stark contrast between John's enthusiasm for the project and some of his colleagues' dismissive attitudes highlighted the very issues the film sought to address, further fueling John's determination to make a difference in the industry.

John's approach to investing is deeply personal. He looks for coachable, humble founders, who are willing to admit what they don't know. "While having a good product that the market wants is important," he emphasizes, "it's about the founder first."

John's journey from successful entrepreneur to champion of women founders illustrates the power of allyship in creating change. By leveraging his position and experience in Silicon Valley, he's working to open doors that have long been closed to women entrepreneurs.

In an industry often criticized for its lack of diversity and inclusion, John Majeski stands out as a catalyst for change. His story serves as a powerful reminder that sometimes, the most impactful disruptions come from within the system itself.

### Connect with John Majeski

# CHAPTER 11

## SMALL TOWN, BIG DREAMS REALIZED

"EVERY OPPORTUNITY **LEADS** TO THE NEXT BLESSING!"

- Julie Peterson Klein

# JULIE PETERSON KLEIN

Investor/Associate Producer

In the heart of North Dakota, a young Julie Peterson Klein dreamed beyond the borders of Milnor, her 700-person hometown. As the youngest of five siblings, Julie wasn't content to simply follow in familial footsteps. Instead, she wove together threads of hard work, community service, and an innate drive to lead, creating a tapestry that would eventually usher her into the world of angel investing.

"My parents always role-modeled working hard and giving back," Julie reflects, her voice echoing small-town values and big-city ambitions. "A lot of times it was volunteering, like through our church." Little did she know that these early lessons in generosity and perseverance would one day fuel her passion for investing in women-led ventures, bridging the gap between her Midwestern roots and the glittering promise of entrepreneurial dreams.

Julie's father played a crucial role in shaping her approach to challenges. "He taught me that you can take any project and break it down and make it simple," she says. This lesson instilled in her the belief that no project is too big to tackle, a mindset that has served her well throughout her career and her investing journey.

Even as a child, Julie displayed natural leadership qualities. She laughs as she remembers coaching her fifth-grade basketball team during a huddle, much to her mother's chagrin. "That was the first time I realized I'm just going to lead, even if I don't know everything about whatever it is," she says. This innate drive, grit, and determination to take charge and make a difference has been a constant thread throughout Julie's life and career.

Julie has always been determined to prove herself. As the youngest in a family of good athletes, "I can remember feeling a lot of pressure when I was young, that I've got to work hard and practice a lot because my older siblings are pretty good at basketball and football and other sports." This early experience of pushing herself to meet high expectations would later translate into her professional life.

After studying business management, Julie joined Bell Bank 25 years ago when it had just 250 employees and $250 million in assets. Today, as Chief Culture Officer and Chief of Staff, she helps lead a company that has grown to over 2,000 employees and $14 billion in assets. Julie's role is to ensure that all employees are "happy, engaged, and believing [in] and carrying out our values here at Bell every single day." She emphasizes the importance of creating a family atmosphere, providing unequaled service, and giving back to communities.

Interestingly, Julie's current position at Bell Bank fulfills a long-held dream. She recalls, "I lived out of town in a different city, but I'd come to Fargo every weekend. I would hit the red light, and I would look up at this building and go, 'Someday I want to work at a big company like that.'" Today, Julie's life and work are living proof of dreams crystallized through unwavering vision and dogged determination, coupled with genuine kindness and humility.

Julie entered angel investing through a serendipitous encounter with Catherine Gray, opening doors to her current investing ventures. As chair of TEDx Fargo, Julie gave a brief introduction, which caught Catherine's attention. "She came right up to me afterward, and we got to know each other," Julie recalls. This chance meeting led to her involvement with *Show Her The Money*, a project that resonated deeply with Julie. She was intrigued by it not just for its potential returns but for its crucial role in educating and empowering women in finance. "The universe brings people into your lives that should be in your life," Julie muses, emphasizing how seemingly small connections can lead to significant opportunities.

For Julie, investing is about more than just financial returns. It's about relationships, learning, and creating positive change. She has since invested in several other projects, including a musical aiming for Broadway and a media company. Each investment opportunity has come through personal connections and a belief in the founders' potential.

"I have to have some sort of a relationship with the people," Julie explains. "I have to see some history of success, and then it would need to be in a passion area, [one] I love and believe in." She emphasizes the importance of doing due diligence and trusting your instincts about people.

Thanks to her diverse experiences, including her work with major award shows in Hollywood, Julie has a unique perspective on the entertainment industry and the power of storytelling. While she's discreet about the details of this work, it's clear that these experiences have broadened her horizons and influenced her approach to investing in creative projects.

Julie's approach to investing aligns with her philosophy of continuous growth and forward momentum. Her word of the year, every year, is "momentum," and her motto is "Every opportunity leads to the next blessing." When asked what advice she would offer aspiring investors, Julie encourages people not to be intimidated by large investment amounts. "Don't be afraid to ask," she urges. "You'll find people more than willing to answer." She also encourages people to get involved by volunteering, networking, and educating themselves, even if they can't invest financially.

Julie reflects, "The universe knew I wasn't ready at a younger age. But I would have started educating myself at a younger age to be ready to go ahead and do it." She hopes that sharing her experiences can inspire others, particularly young women, to learn about investing earlier in life.

As for the future, Julie is excited about the potential impact of *Show Her The Money* and related initiatives. "Just think of the generations," she says, envisioning the ripple effects of educating more women about investing. "You get a whole bunch of women behind a movement; you better watch out."

Julie's path from small-town dreamer to respected business leader and angel investor is truly inspiring, illuminating the possibilities for women everywhere to dream big, work hard, and continually move forward.

### Connect with Julie Peterson Klein

# FEMALE-DRIVEN CROWDFUNDING CAMPAIGNS TEND TO OUTPERFORM THOSE LED BY MEN, OBTAINING 1.3 TIMES MORE CONTRIBUTORS AND SECURING 10.75% MORE FUNDING.

Source: PwC and The Crowdfunding Centre

# CHAPTER 12

## MULTI-MILLION DOLLAR EXIT-THINKING BIGGER

"IF YOU WANT TO GO FAST, GO ALONE. IF YOU WANT TO GO FAR, GO TOGETHER."

- African Proverb

## SARAH DUSEK

Investor/Associate Producer

"I sold my business for over $100 million, if I can do it, you can too." Sarah Dusek's journey from aid worker to glamping entrepreneur to venture capitalist showcases the power of thinking big and the importance of women supporting women in business. Her story begins in the nonprofit world, where she spent a decade working for NGOs in Africa and the Far East. Little did she know that this experience would lay the foundation for a groundbreaking business venture and ultimately lead her to become a champion for female founders.

In 2009, Sarah and her husband, both former aid workers with no business experience, reimagined their future on his family's farm in Montana. Inspired by Sarah's love for African safaris, they hatched an idea to recreate the safari experience for an American audience. Armed with a dream and determination, they set up four tents and a dining area on the family farm. "We spent our inheritance on making that happen," Sarah recalls. "And boom, complete failure."

While their original concept didn't attract guests, it did spark interest in their unique tents. "The phone would ring, and people would ask us, 'Where did you get your tents? They're so amazing. They're so beautiful.' And we would say, well, they are, and you can come and stay with us right here. But nobody wanted to stay in the middle of the prairie in Montana." Through several pivots, Sarah and her husband eventually landed on Under Canvas, a winning formula of luxury tented resorts near national parks across the US that would pioneer the glamping industry in America.

Sarah and her husband bootstrapped their business for six years, reinvesting profits and incurring some debt to fuel growth. However, increasing competition in the industry made them eager to find a solution to scale more rapidly. Then, as if by fate, a female venture capitalist came and stayed at one of their properties, fell in love with the concept, and introduced Sarah and her husband to the world of outside investment.

"She was super helpful. She sent me some examples of what decks look like, how to build a deck, what kind of things go in your deck, what kind of metrics investors are looking for, and how to think about pitching to investors. I was so naive. I didn't even know that people got investments for growing and scaling companies," Sarah admits. "That just wasn't on my radar."

This introduction to venture capital opened Sarah's eyes to new possibilities, but it also exposed her to the challenges women face in securing funding. Her first encounter with a potential investor left her disillusioned. The terms were predatory, threatening to strip her of control despite only offering a minority stake. "It was so disappointing," Sarah remembers. "I thought, 'Oh, investors help you.' Not so much."

This experience became a defining moment for Sarah. She vowed that if she ever built a valuable company, she would become the kind of investor she had been looking for—one who championed founders and sought win-win scenarios.

Sarah's perseverance paid off. In 2017, she secured the investment she needed to scale Under Canvas. Just a year later, a major buyer approached her with an offer to purchase the company. The decision to sell was emotionally challenging, but it began an exciting new chapter in Sarah's career.

True to her word, Sarah founded Enygma Ventures in 2019, a venture capital fund focused exclusively on investing in female founders. Her mission: to address the funding gap for women entrepreneurs and help them think bigger from the start. "One of the biggest problems that women tend to have is they tend to think too small," Sarah observes. "I'm constantly saying to women, 'What would it take to think about building a $100 million business?'" She writes about this in her book *Think Bigger* in an effort to help women reach their highest level of success.

Sarah's experience as both a founder and now an investor has given her unique insights into the challenges women face in the business world. She notes that women often approach risk differently than men, playing it safer and possibly limiting their growth potential.

"There's no way you win big if you don't risk everything," Sarah asserts. "Some of these approaches to how you think about risk, how you win—all of that stuff is much more problematic for women than it tends to be for men."

Through Enygma Ventures, Sarah is working to change this mindset and empower women to think bigger. She looks for founders who can envision scale and are willing to take the necessary risks to achieve it. However, she's acutely aware of the uphill battle in changing perceptions within the investment community.

"Selling women as an investable asset class is tough," Sarah admits. "But our fund is three and a half times more valuable than when we started. I have absolutely no doubt that our fund will perform above and beyond my male counterparts."

Sarah's passion for empowering women in business extends beyond her work with Enygma Ventures. When she heard about the documentary, *Show Her The Money*, she immediately recognized its potential to inspire and educate. "That title right there is everything I'm about, everything I'm trying to do," Sarah explains. "Every story I want to tell is about getting more money into the hands of women, helping other female entrepreneurs do that, and understanding what that takes."

Looking back on her journey, Sarah wishes she had raised capital earlier and in larger amounts as a founder. As an investor, she continues to face challenges in fundraising for her women-focused fund but remains committed to her mission. And in Few & Far Luvhondo, her newest venture, she transforms the luxury safari into an experience that inspires both awe and awareness, putting conservation and rebuilding the local community and environment at the forefront.

Sarah's story powerfully reminds us of the importance of representation and diversity in the investment world. As she puts it, "Nothing bad happens when women have economic substance and economic power. Children are educated. Schools are built. Communities are built. Our communities thrive because we are so much more focused on everything that's going on around us, not just our little selves and our little worlds."

For Sarah, the path forward is clear: More women need to step into the role of investor to create a more diverse and equitable funding landscape. She hopes that by sharing her story and supporting other women, she can help create a world where female founders have equal access to capital and opportunities.

As she looks to the future, Sarah remains guided by the African proverb she holds dear: "If you want to go fast, go alone. If you want to go far, go together." In her view, this encapsulates the essence of the women's empowerment movement in business—a collective journey towards systemic change that can only be achieved by working together.

<h2 style="text-align:center;color:#ff3399;">Connect with Sarah Dusek</h2>

# CHAPTER 13

# LAUNCHING A VENTURE FUND

**"LET YOURSELF BE SILENTLY DRAWN BY THE STRANGE PULL OF WHAT YOU REALLY LOVE. IT WILL NOT LEAD YOU ASTRAY."**

- Rumi

# LA KEISHA LANDRUM PIERRE

Investor/Associate Producer/Supporting Cast

La Keisha Landrum Pierre's path to becoming a venture capitalist began not in the bustling hills of Silicon Valley, but in the sun-soaked streets of Orange County, California. As a child, while her peers were focused on local adventures, La Keisha's world was expanding far beyond her suburban borders.

"From a very young age, my parents did a great job of helping me understand that my connection to humanity meant I'm connected to my neighbors—the person who lives next door to me, and my neighbor is the person who lives in Chad, in Nairobi, in Paris," La Keisha reflects. This early exposure to a world without boundaries laid the foundation for a global perspective and diverse network of friends and colleagues spanning many corners of the world. La Keisha's journey from a globally-minded child to a pioneering force in venture capital is a glowing example of the power of perspective and perseverance, and the belief that profit and purpose can go hand in hand.

The entrepreneurial spirit modeled by her family truly set La Keisha on her path. Her aunt provided a powerful influence through her own business. "As a very little girl, watching my aunt build out a real estate brokerage firm, go look at a property, buy it, and then roll my mom into it and buy apartment buildings, and then watch them build wealth—that entrepreneurship is a big part of my upbringing," La Keisha says. These early visuals made starting and building a business seem not just possible but natural. At 18, she obtained her real estate license and began working under her aunt's brokerage, gaining firsthand experience in deal-making and client relations.

Her global mindset, cultivated from childhood, led La Keisha to co-found Sahara Reporters, one of the largest international media companies focused on Africa. This venture proved transformative, allowing her to pursue her passion for storytelling while challenging her to balance social impact with profitability. "I wanted to prove that you can have a social impact and also be profitable. And we did prove that out," La Keisha states proudly. The experience honed La Keisha's ability to identify and nurture impactful ventures, cultivating skills that would become invaluable in her future role as a venture capitalist.

La Keisha's entry into venture capital came as a natural expansion of the family-level investments she and her husband made for several years through her family office, the Pierre Family Fund. "I made a personal shift coming out of the pandemic to say, I ought to really take my talents and what I've done and take it to that next level, giving myself permission to do something different. And so I joined an organization that's designed to bring more women into investing."

There, she met her future co-founders. "We were put on the same deal team. We looked at the same company and conducted due diligence on it together. We really loved working together and so we decided, let's pool our capital and invest together in 14 female-led companies," La Keisha recounts. This "pilot fund" was the precursor to Emmeline Ventures, allowing them to test their collaborative dynamic and refine their investment thesis.

"We realized we were onto something," La Keisha reflects. "There was a clear gap: women eager to invest, but unsure how, and brilliant women entrepreneurs building great businesses but struggling to access capital. We saw an opportunity to be that crucial connection point."

Encouraged by their success and recognizing this significant market need, they took the leap to launch Emmeline Ventures. This early-stage venture capital firm focuses on healthcare, financial services, and sustainability solutions built by women—areas deliberately chosen to reflect both societal needs and sectors where women founders are making significant strides.

The transition from individual investors to VC firm founders was challenging. "It's a lot of work," La Keisha emphasizes. Despite the legal, regulatory, and networking hurdles, their conviction in the need for such a firm only grew stronger. They saw themselves as nurturing an ecosystem, creating that bridge between aspiring women investors and women entrepreneurs who needed their support.

For new investors, La Keisha strongly advises partnering with an established fund. "You just shouldn't do it alone," she insists. "It's so much work to properly conduct due diligence on a company, and unless you're doing this as a full-time job or partner with people who are making it their full-time job, you won't be able to do the level of work that you need to really understand a business."

When evaluating founders, La Keisha and her team at Emmeline employ a unique due diligence process that focuses heavily on founder alignment. "Is this founder matched to the project that they're going to take to completion?" she asks. They assess not just the business idea, but whether the founder has the necessary skills, time commitment, and resilience to see it through.

"If you actually practice the art of finding strategically aligned individuals early on, you'll kiss fewer frogs," she advises, likening making an investment to embarking on an intimate, long-term relationship. "You're like beginning some version of a marriage, a business marriage," she says. "And it's been a tough lesson to really understand—yeah, you're in this for the long haul."

One of Emmeline's distinguishing features is their hands-on approach with portfolio companies. "We work very closely with founders," La Keisha explains. "We're having regular calls with them. We're understanding what their needs are. We're understanding how to be supportive." This high-touch strategy helps de-risk investments in an underserved market of women entrepreneurs who receive only a fraction of total venture capital.

La Keisha recalls one of their early investments, a healthcare startup founded by a woman with deep industry expertise but limited entrepreneurial experience. Emmeline's team worked closely with the founder, helping her refine her pitch, make key hires, and navigate her first major contract negotiations. This hands-on approach not only helped the company secure additional funding but also accelerated its path to market.

When asked about her best investment to date, La Keisha doesn't hesitate: "The best investment I made today is the investment in myself." By investing in herself to join a network of women investors, she set in motion the chain of events that led to Emmeline Ventures and their subsequent investments in 25 incredible founders and counting.

Another hard-won lesson has been realizing that the principles they teach their founders apply equally to themselves as investors. "The lessons that you're teaching and working on with your founders are the same lessons for you," La Keisha reflects. "They can't quit just because things have gotten really, really difficult, or they've hit a major wrinkle. Those principles are ours, too."

For founders seeking investment, La Keisha offers this advice: "Engage early and often at a time when you don't need the capital. Build such that when you do need the capital, the relationships are teed up." She notes that approaching investors from a place of desperation often yields different results than building relationships when you're in a strong position.

As for the future, La Keisha is optimistic about the growing role of women in venture capital. She's particularly excited about companies that are addressing systemic issues in healthcare, financial inclusion, and sustainability. "We're seeing incredible innovations from women founders who are solving problems they've experienced firsthand," she notes. "These are the companies that have the potential to create real, lasting change."

La Keisha's journey from a globally minded child of entrepreneurs to a pioneering venture capitalist demonstrates the power of early exposure, personal investment, and a commitment to changing narratives and creating opportunities for underserved founders. "Each investment we make is a step towards changing the face of entrepreneurship and venture capital," La Keisha concludes. "We're not just building companies; we're building a new paradigm of what's possible when we invest in diverse founders and ideas."

## Connect with La Keisha Landrum Pierre

# CHAPTER 14

# RESHAPING EARLY STAGE INVESTING

# "NEVER UNDERESTIMATE THE POWER WE WOMEN HAVE TO DEFINE OUR OWN DESTINIES."

- Emmeline Pankhurst

## AZIN RADSAN VAN ALEBEEK

Investor/Associate Producer/Supporting Cast

Maverick investor Azin Radsan van Alebeek's journey to the pinnacle of venture capital reads like a playbook for defying expectations. Born to Iranian immigrants, Azin's path began at a boutique consulting firm then wound through years as a stay-at-home mom and community volunteer before leading to her current role as Co-Founder of Emmeline Ventures. Now, she harnesses her diverse life experiences to reshape early-stage investing, laser-focused on empowering women and historically excluded entrepreneurs in an industry known for its homogeneity.

Growing up Iranian in a small Michigan town, Azin stood out as one of only two children who didn't look like everyone else. Rather than letting this difference hold her back, "I just leaned in," she recalls, "and almost disregarded the fact that I wasn't like the others. I was like, 'I'm just gonna do my own thing and find positions of power.'" Her early experience of being different shaped her approach to life, instilling a sense of independence and a willingness to forge her own path.

Azin's fascination with finance sparked early. "I've always liked money," she admits. "I've always understood that money is power, that money is a tool that you use to obtain access." As a teenager, she began to grasp the power of the stock market, listening intently to her father's discussions about investing. Her interest deepened when she realized her father was building her a custodial account.

Azin fondly remembers receiving her first paper stock certificate, a tangible symbol of her budding connection to the financial world. After college, Azin's career trajectory seemed set. She worked in consulting, interacting with C-level executives and boards of directors. However, life had other plans. When she became pregnant with her first child, Azin decided to step out of the workforce to become a stay-at-home mom.

This pivot surprised many—even Azin herself. "My high school class had voted me least likely to become a mother," she laughs. Yet, true to her nature, "If you're going to put me in a role, I'm going to do it well,", "So now I'm going to be the best stay-at-home mom ever."

For 25 years, Azin dedicated herself to raising her children and supporting her family. During this time, she continued to learn and grow, taking on volunteer projects and roles that allowed her to upskill and stay engaged. She taught art in public schools, served on advisory committees, and even learned Dutch when her family moved to the Netherlands.

Throughout her years as a stay-at-home mom, Azin maintained her connection to the world of finance through personal investing. She made her first angel investment in 2008, keeping one foot in the door of the financial world even as she focused on her family. This experience helped her refine what she calls an "investor mindset"—maintaining a long-term view, making data-driven decisions, and remaining emotionally disciplined.

When Azin later got divorced, she approached this trying time with the same principles she had honed through years of investing. "I kept front and center in my mind that this was all about making sure that assets were split well, that it was fair, and that when our children were getting married and having children, we could be in the room together."

Her approach to the divorce exemplified how she had successfully applied her investor mindset to personal challenges. Azin navigated this difficult period with remarkable clarity and purpose by maintaining emotional discipline and focusing on long-term outcomes.

In 2020, Azin participated in an investor boot camp, where she met her future co-founders of Emmeline Ventures, Naseem Sayani and La Keisha Landrum Pierre. The boot camp's mission to bring more women and people of color into venture capital resonated deeply with her. As she collaborated with her future partners, she realized their collective potential: "Where one plus one plus one was seven, and not three."

Launched in April 2022, Emmeline Ventures focuses on early-stage investments in sectors that can help women live and thrive. Inspired by British suffragette Emmeline Pankhurst, the firm's name reflects its mission to buck narratives, break rules, and change tides.

As a general partner, Azin brings her unique perspective and varied life experiences to evaluate potential investments. She seeks a rare combination of passion, innovation, and adaptability. "I look for founders who share a passion and understanding of the problem they're trying to solve," she explains. "They need to be fired up about both the problem and their solution."

Azin values disruptive thinking over incremental improvements. "Don't give me a bandaid," she asserts. "Re-engineer it from the beginning."

Today, Azin views her participation in the venture capital space not just as a career choice but as a moral imperative. As a woman privileged to enter this arena, she feels a profound responsibility to drive change. As Azin dug into the data, she uncovered a shocking truth that galvanized her mission: "When I came out of college in 1988, that was a whole different world, you could say. Except data shows that the representation of women in the workforce and our ability to access childcare, senior care, or any of these things that really are important to women are the same today as they were for students coming out of college then. And that is appalling."

Ultimately, Azin has positioned herself to impact the world of venture capital significantly. As she puts it, "I am doing this in my third chapter because I can. And if I don't do it, who else will?"

Through Emmeline Ventures, Azin works tirelessly to democratize venture capital, aiming to reshape an industry long dominated by a homogeneous group. Her mission extends beyond mere representation; she seeks to fundamentally alter the landscape of early-stage investing ensuring that innovative ideas from all corners of society have a fair shot at success.

**Connect with Azin Radsan van Alebeek**

# CHAPTER 15

# HELPING WOMEN GROW AND SCALE

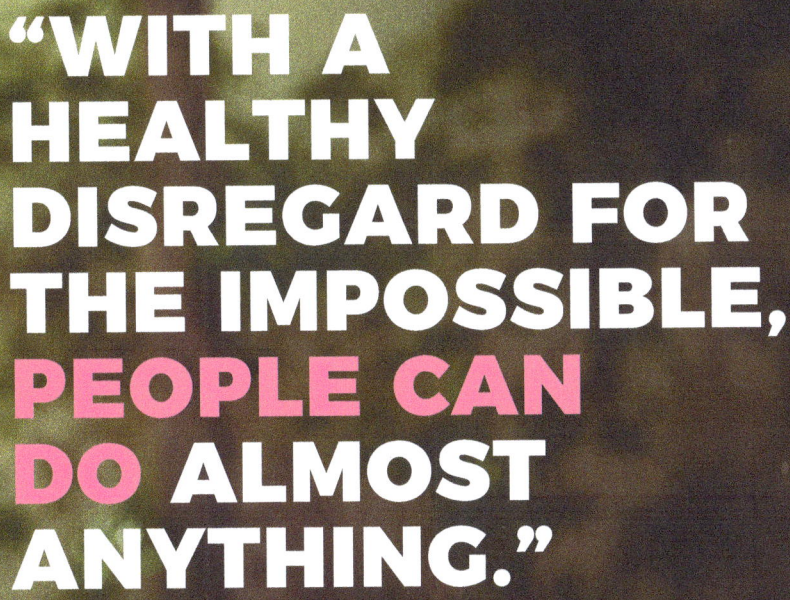

**"WITH A HEALTHY DISREGARD FOR THE IMPOSSIBLE, PEOPLE CAN DO ALMOST ANYTHING."**

- Larry Page

## NASEEM SAYANI

Investor/Associate Producer/Supporting Cast

At the intersection of innovation and entrepreneurship, Naseem Sayani's journey from a tradition-bound South Asian household to becoming a formidable venture capitalist exemplifies the transformative power of resilience and unwavering determination. Her story is a testament to the impact of challenging societal norms and pursuing one's vision of empowerment. Naseem's narrative is one of defiance, dedication, and an unrelenting commitment to creating opportunities for women in business.

Born in Southern California to immigrant parents from India, Naseem's upbringing was steeped in cultural expectations that often clashed with her innate curiosity and desire for self-determination. "I was always asking questions. 'Why do I have to learn to cook?' 'Why doesn't Dad cook?' 'Why do I have to dress a certain way?'" she recalls, her voice carrying echoes of a rebellion that would shape her future endeavors.

After graduating from UCLA with a degree in economics and a minor in computer science, Naseem embarked on a successful career in technology consulting, quickly climbing the ranks at firms like Arthur Andersen Business Consulting and IBM. She then went to business school in New York and transitioned into digital strategy and innovation consulting, joining Booz & Company in 2007—the same year many of us first had iPhones in our hands. From there, her entrepreneurial spirit truly took flight when, around 2011, her team at Booz & Company launched an innovative product studio called Booz Digital to help clients not just strategize but actively build and test products in the market.

"It wasn't enough to do the strategy work because they couldn't execute on it," Naseem explains. "So we launched a product studio to help them turn on experiences, build apps, and test things in-market." This bold move allowed Naseem and her colleagues to work directly with clients, using their resources to launch startups that could disrupt incumbents rather than be disrupted themselves.

Within four years, that product studio had evolved into a full-fledged startup incubator, a game-changing endeavor that deepened Naseem's passion for supporting innovative founders and businesses. During this transformative period, Naseem's commitment to empowering women entrepreneurs took root. Recognizing a dearth of female founders and women of color in the startup ecosystem, she began actively seeking them out. "I was specifically looking for female founders who were building new businesses that I wouldn't have met via my day job."

One of her earliest and likely most successful angel investments was in a sustainable period care company called August, which she backed during its pre-seed round. "Their valuation was sub $5 million. When they got to their seed, it was at $21 million. And they've been growing like crazy," Naseem shares, her voice brimming with pride.

As her angel portfolio grew, Naseem met her future co-founders, Azin Radsan van Alebeek and La Keisha Landrum Pierre. The trio quickly recognized their shared ethos and desire to create meaningful change through investment. In 2019, they launched their pilot fund, crystallizing their focus on female founders and the businesses they were building.

"We wanted to make sure that they also had capital and ecosystem support so that they could grow and build a business, secure an exit, and do all the things that their white male counterparts are doing quite easily," Naseem explains, her words underscoring the urgency of their mission.

Two and a half years later, Emmeline Ventures was born, a full-fledged venture fund dedicated to investing in women's health, financial services, and sustainability—sectors where technology and innovation can profoundly impact women's lives.

At the core of Emmeline's investment philosophy is a deep respect for the founders they back and a commitment to fostering long-term partnerships. "We want to know we can spend time together," Naseem says. "We can talk business, we can also go have dinner and talk about our kids or weekend plans. We can be friends while also being business partners."

One of the most essential lessons Naseem has learned is the importance of trusting her own "sniff test" when evaluating potential investments, rather than relying solely on signals from others. "We can't rely on someone else's decision to invest. We have to make sure we can hang our hat on it also," she asserts, highlighting the rigorous due diligence required to build a robust portfolio.

Looking ahead, Naseem envisions a venture capital landscape that mirrors society's diversity, where investment decisions are made through a lens of inclusivity and equity. "Women who run businesses outperform their male peers 15 to 30 percent," she points out, highlighting the untapped potential and financial upside of supporting women-led ventures.

Naseem recently expanded her focus by making the leap to join How Women Invest as an Operating Advisor and Venture Partner for Fund III. How Women Invest Fund III is a $100M fund investing in 100% female-founded teams at Series A and B across healthcare, climate, and the future of work.

"Women have founded some of the most significant companies in these categories, especially at the intersection of generative AI," Naseem shared, "Fund III adds significant capital to this growth." Naseem is leading overall strategy, deal flow, and sourcing and also sits on the investment committee. "This role also gives me incredible access to actionable policy and regulatory influence, which will be critical to advancing the women-led VC and founder ecosystem in the coming years."

Naseem's mission is a clarion call to reclaim the power of community—a superpower that women have historically wielded to build cities and nations. "If we all stood up and made decisions about our money—how we save it, how we spend it, how we invest it—in ways that were coordinated, the whole world would change," she declares, her words carrying the weight of a revolution in the making.

In today's world, where venture capital has an outsized influence on shaping behaviors and driving innovation, Naseem is determined to ensure that women's voices and perspectives are not just heard but amplified. Through her investments, mentorship, and advocacy, she is not only changing individual lives but also encouraging a broader movement toward gender equality in business.

"I'm working harder than I ever have," Naseem shares with passion. "It's about helping women grow and scale and witnessing their success." Her legacy is one of unwavering support and achievement, a testament to unyielding determination for meaningful impact.

## Connect with Naseem Sayani

# CHAPTER 16

---

# INVESTING
# WITH DONOR
# ADVISORY
# FUNDS

**"ONLY DO WHAT ONLY YOU CAN DO."**

- Paul Sloane

**REBECCA HART**

Investor/Associate Producer

Growing up in a household where financial caution reigned supreme, it's taken a lot for Rebecca Hart to become the angel investor she is today. "I have had to work very, very hard to overcome 'scarcity mentality'," she reflects. Her early conditioning and later career in the PR industry made her an unlikely candidate for the high-risk world of angel investing. Yet, it ultimately led her to develop a unique approach to investing for her family that balances financial returns with social impact.

Rebecca Hart's journey into angel investing tells a story of transformation—from a child of Depression-era parents who instilled a "save, save, save" mentality to changing the landscape of philanthropy and impact investing. Her path demonstrates how personal growth, innovative thinking, and a commitment to social impact can converge to create meaningful change in finance and beyond.

Rebecca's first experiences with angel investing began while attempting to invest in an impact fund through her local Community Foundation. With a vision to grow the fund, Rebecca started exploring innovative ways to maximize their philanthropic impact. "If this is something that I want my children to be able to participate in, we need it to have some healthy growth," she explains.

Driven by this goal, Rebecca completed a fellowship with Impact Finance Center and joined a "Learn by Doing" group to understand the mechanics of due diligence and investing. This pivotal decision introduced her to Next Wave Impact, and the group's investment committee, where she met experienced investors, connections that would prove instrumental in shaping Rebecca's investing journey and philosophy.

Through her involvement with Next Wave, Rebecca began to see the potential for using the foundation's funds more impactfully. However, she quickly encountered resistance when proposing alternative investment strategies to the Community Foundation. "I asked in multiple ways: 'Can I invest in an impact fund instead of the stock market? Can we take some part and invest in a local entrepreneur?' The answer was 'no'."

Undeterred by this setback, Rebecca set out to educate herself and find innovative ways to achieve her vision. Her persistence led her to a game-changing discovery for angel investing: using donor-advised funds—also known as DAF. She discovered these are charitable giving accounts where donors can contribute assets, receive an immediate tax deduction, and then recommend grants to charities over time, allowing for flexibility in their philanthropic efforts.

This revelation would transform her approach to philanthropy and investing, allowing her to overcome her ingrained financial caution and enter the world of high-impact, mission-driven investing.

"I would not have the courage to do this work without using donor-advised funds," Rebecca explains. "I tell people if you have a DAF and you want to do this work, don't take 'no' for an answer. You can transfer funds to a provider who will facilitate impact investments." The mental shift freed her to take risks she might not have considered with personal funds, opening up a world of possibilities for supporting innovative, impact-driven businesses.

Rebecca made the first investment for her family in the summer of 2016, marking the beginning of her active involvement in angel investing. Since then, she has built a diverse portfolio of more than 25 investments, always focusing on companies that offer more than just financial returns.

Her journey in impact investing led her to involvement with *Show Her The Money*. Rebecca's connection to the film came through her network of fellow investors. "I saw that they were investing in the movie," she recalls. "And I thought, 'Hey, I want to do that too.'"

The film resonated with Rebecca on multiple levels. With her background in broadcast journalism and PR, she saw it as an opportunity to return to her roots. "More storytelling, more investing, and more documentaries," she explains. "That's what I want to do."

The film's focus on women investors supporting women-led businesses aligned perfectly with Rebecca's own investment philosophy. Her involvement with the film has allowed her to support an important project and connected her with a broader community of like-minded investors, including Catherine Gray.

Rebecca's approach to investing remains deeply rooted in the concept of impact. She aligns her investments with the United Nations Sustainable Development goals. "I was always looking for and still am always looking for some kind of impact measures that go beyond the financial return," she says.

One of her favorite investments illustrates this approach perfectly. Motivo, a platform she describes as "match.com for therapists," addresses the critical shortage of mental health professionals by connecting therapists-in-training with supervisors. The impact resonates clearly: increasing access to mental health services in underserved areas. "Are we going to have a good financial return? Hopefully. But in the meantime, very important impact measures are being accomplished," Rebecca explains.

Her focus on impact ties directly back to her use of donor-advised funds. As she puts it, "Would we have made a grant to accomplish what they're trying to accomplish?" The question serves as a guiding principle, helping her navigate the complex world of impact investing while staying true to the philanthropic spirit of her funds. "The goal is a good financial return; however, if that doesn't happen, it's the same result as if we made a grant. So whatever we earn back beats a grant."

Her wisdom has shaped her approach to due diligence, deal selection, and understanding the complexities of deal structures and exit scenarios. "I naively thought [that] if you have the first money in, you're at an advantage because you took the most risk," she admits. "It's not like that."

One of the most valuable lessons she's learned along the way emphasizes the importance of focusing on founders with a clear exit strategy. "If the founder isn't focused on an exit, you might be funding a lifestyle business," she advises. "If so, you may support the entrepreneur and accomplish some impact, but you're probably not going to get a return on that money. So you need a winner to offset that loss."

Rebecca offers clear advice for founders seeking investment: Stay focused on the exit, communicate your impact measures, and actively engage your investors in supporting your business. "Make sure your investors know about opportunities to help," she urges. "Because we have a vested interest in helping to promote you."

Rebecca has maintained a commitment to pushing boundaries and challenging conventional thinking about impact investing throughout her investing journey. From exploring the environmental benefits of boxed wine to supporting menopause-focused fintech, she continually seeks to expand the definition of what constitutes impactful investing. Her innovative approach has earned her a reputation as a "Southern Disruptor" who can walk into a room and effect change without raising immediate resistance.

Looking to the future, Rebecca champions the vast, untapped potential of donor-advised funds. She recalls a colleague's striking perspective that deeply resonated with her: "This is sacred money. You made a deal when you agreed not to pay tax on this money. Letting it sit in the stock market is not upholding your part of the bargain." Rebecca has passionately adopted this view, arguing that the billions of dollars in donor-advised funds nationwide must be put to work. For Rebecca, this concept represents not just an opportunity, but a responsibility to maximize the impact of these philanthropic resources.

As Rebecca continues to navigate the complex world of impact investing, she remains guided by a simple yet powerful quote: "Only do what only you can do." In her case, that means pushing boundaries, challenging conventions, and finding innovative ways to use financial resources for maximum social impact.

## Connect with Rebecca Hart

**100-CITY WORLDWIDE TOUR**

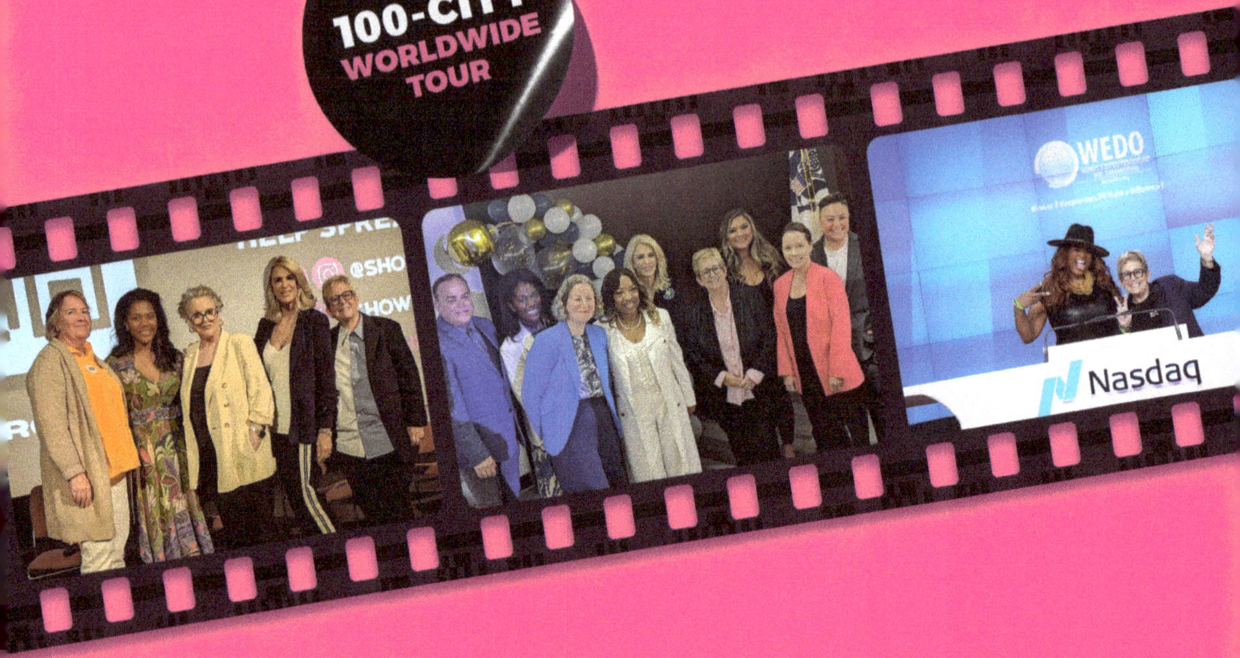

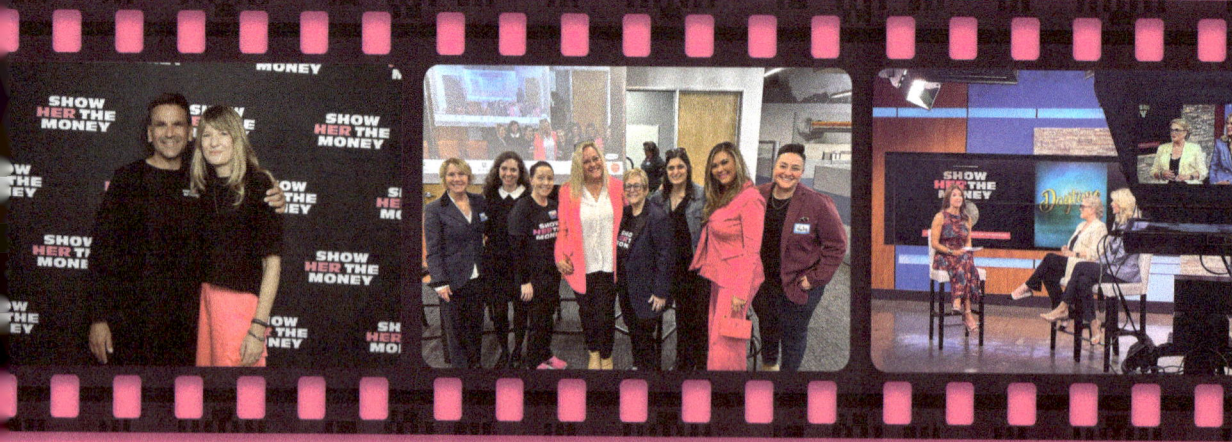

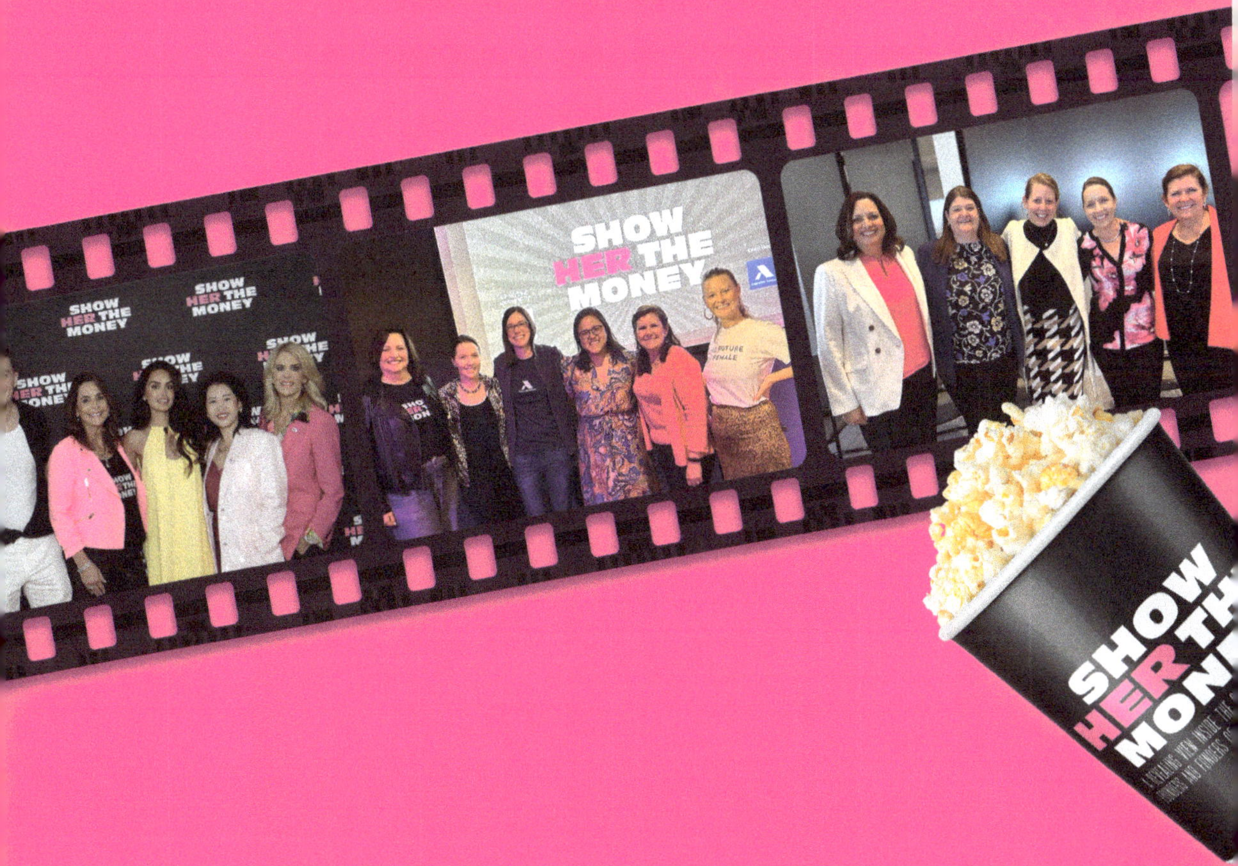
SHOW HER THE MONEY

SHOW HER THE MONEY

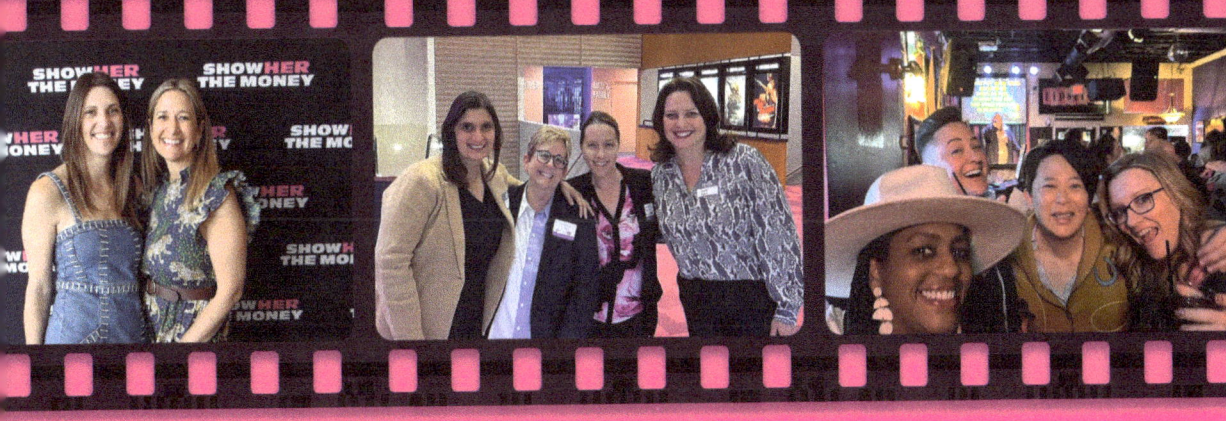

# CHAPTER 17

# FOSTERING POSITIVE CHANGE

**"I HAVE LEARNED THAT PEOPLE WILL FORGET WHAT YOU SAID, PEOPLE WILL FORGET WHAT YOU DID, BUT PEOPLE WILL NEVER FORGET HOW YOU MADE THEM FEEL."**

- Maya Angelou

# SONDRA SMALLEY

Investor/Associate Producer

At 89 years young, Sondra Smalley is rewriting the rulebook on making a difference in the world. Born in the city of Los Angeles, Sondra's life has been a tapestry of love, family, and giving back. But her recent foray into the investment world has added an exciting new chapter to her already remarkable story.

Raised in the San Fernando Valley, Sondra grew up in what she calls "the great generation," a time of unlocked doors and childhood freedom. Her family's commitment to community support was ingrained early on. Her grandfather, David Familian, was one of the founders of the City of Hope and her parents contributed generously to the American Jewish University, for whom the campus was named: The Sunny and Isadore Familian Campus—though as of 2024, that campus belongs to The Milken Community School.

Sondra's own story of love began early. She met her husband, Marvin Smalley, at 14, married at 17, and enjoyed a 70-year marriage that brought them four children, seven grandchildren, and two great-grandchildren. Throughout their lives together, Sondra and Marvin continued the family tradition of philanthropic support, focusing on nonprofit organizations. "Supporting nonprofits has been my mission and I have tried to teach that to my children and grandchildren," she explains. These philanthropic institutions include Cedars Sinai Medical Center, St. John's Health Center, MOCA, Music Center of Los Angeles, The Los Angeles Jewish Federation, The Holocaust Museum, Aviva Family and Children's Services (The Wallace Home), She Angels Foundation, Mothers 2 Mothers, and Beit T' Shuvah.

However, Sondra's approach to giving has evolved, particularly since her husband's passing three years ago. Her daughter, Debra Smalley, notes a significant change: "When dad passed away, my mom underwent a metamorphosis. She's had to take care of everything now. And I'm so impressed. Seeing the growth in these three years is remarkable and commendable."

This growth includes Sondra's first foray into investment through her support of *Show Her The Money*. Sondra found Catherine's enthusiasm and vision compelling and exciting—and it's not just because Catherine also happens to be her daughter-in-law.

"From the first time I met Catherine, I said, 'Wow, she brings love and happiness to my daughter and our family,'" Sondra recalls. "Because I have so much confidence in Catherine, that is the reason that I invested with her. She is creative and smart. She puts people together who have never met, and boom, they have something in common. She has that intuition."

Sondra's decision to invest in the film marks a notable shift from her traditional philanthropic approach. "I think that as a result of this film that she has invested in and supported, she's looking at things from a different lens," Debra observes.

This new outlook has changed Sondra's perspective about the power of investment, especially in supporting women entrepreneurs and innovators. "I think what Debra said is correct, investing in something such as this film, has opened my eyes to something different, something I can do on my own," Sondra reflects. "I think investing in this film, watching the positive influence it has had on this asset class, and being a part of it, has kept me even younger."

Sondra's venture into the investment world has ignited a passion for her support of women's leadership. "I think women have a different sensibility and point of view, a different way of thinking," she reflects. "And I think we would have a better world if more women ran more companies." This evolving mindset showcases how her involvement with *Show Her The Money* goes beyond financial support; it's reshaping her views on women's capacity to revolutionize industries and society. Sondra now sees investments as a powerful tool for fostering positive global change through diverse female leadership.

Despite her age, Sondra maintains an active lifestyle that would put many younger individuals to shame. For the past 28 years, she has worked out with the same trainer three times a week. She gardens daily, plays canasta to keep her mind sharp, and is intentional about reaching out to at least five people each month to maintain connections.

She also remains committed to her philanthropic efforts. Sondra and her late husband, Marvin, established the Sondra and Marvin Smalley Sculpture Garden, a public art installation at American Jewish University, featuring works by renowned artists. This project, dedicated in 1981, exemplifies the couple's commitment to enriching their community through art and culture.

Sondra Smalley's story is one of continuous growth and adaptation. From her early days of traditional philanthropy to adding her current foray into investment, she exemplifies the idea that it's always possible to learn, grow, and make a difference. Her involvement with *Show Her The Money* supports a vital project and represents a personal evolution in how she approaches making an impact.

Through Sondra Smalley's lifelong commitment to giving and her newfound enthusiasm for investing in women entrepreneurs, she hopes to influence how other women from her generation perceive it.

# BY 2030, WOMEN IN THE U.S. WILL CONTROL APPROXIMATELY $34 TRILLION, NEARLY DOUBLING THEIR SHARE OF INVESTABLE ASSETS FROM A DECADE PRIOR.

Source: Projections by McKinsey & Company

# CHAPTER 18

# INVESTING
# TO CREATE
# AN IMPACT

"**DON'T JUST WAIT FOR LIFE TO HAPPEN—JUMP IN WITH PURPOSE. REAL CHANGE HAPPENS WHEN YOU TAKE BOLD ACTION, LIVE FULLY, AND LEAD WITH INTENTION.**"

- Stella Lim

## STELLA LIM
Investor/Associate Producer

Stella Lim's path from a curious girl in Jakarta to a trailblazing angel investor illuminates the transformative power of personal experience. As an advocate for women-led businesses in the male-dominated realm of venture capital, she is an inspiration of hope and possibility, reshaping the landscape of investment one bold decision at a time.

Stella's childhood in Indonesia was full of contrasts, weaving together moments of unbridled freedom and subtle societal constraints. She fondly remembers riding bikes with neighborhood children when gender distinctions seemed nonexistent. However, her parents challenged this idyllic sense of equality when they sent her younger brother to Singapore for better educational opportunities—a privilege not extended to her. "At the time, I was like, 'Oh, okay. That's weird, but I guess it is what it is,'" Stella recalls, pinpointing this moment when she first recognized gender inequity in her world.

Stella's groundbreaking journey into male-dominated industries began at 17, when she boldly moved from Jakarta to the United States for school before returning to Asia. She then spent 18 years in Jakarta, Singapore, Bali, and Sydney, Australia, building a successful career in the energy sector. "I began my career when I joined the family engineering business. A decade later, I was named Director and grew the business into multiple successful ventures." Stella often found herself the only woman in boardrooms dominated by men, and her awareness of this imbalance laid the foundation for her future advocacy for women in business and investing.

Things took a sudden turn, however, when an unexpected cancer diagnosis jolted Stella into reevaluating her life and career trajectory. "I had to reassess my priorities," Stella explains, so she stepped back from her company's operations. "I underwent major surgery, and the chemotherapy took a significant toll on me both physically and mentally."

Stella's health struggle revealed a harsh reality: the ability to prioritize one's well-being over work is a privilege not afforded to everyone. This awareness lit her fire for supporting other women. "Thankfully, I beat cancer. I began my impact investing journey before my cancer diagnosis, but after the health struggle, I started AM Diversity Ventures as a vehicle to steer investments into underfunded communities," she explains.

A startling realization marked Stella's entry into angel investing. At an investment dinner, she was the lone woman. "At dinner, I found myself among 19 male investors discussing deal flow and it struck me how important it is for women to be included at this table too!" "I was like, 'What is this dinner?' 'Why are there no women at this dinner?'" she recalls. The obvious imbalance prompted her to question the lack of diversity in the investment landscape and to take action.

Determined to make a difference, Stella began actively seeking out and supporting diverse businesses. Stella had recently served on the Board of Directors for the Golden Gate Business Association, supporting efforts to drive economic and social progress in the Bay Area and became actively involved in several female-focused angel networks and venture firms. She expanded her focus to include a broader range of underrepresented entrepreneurs. As she puts it, "I needed to really focus on having minority, BIPOC, and LGBTQ women founders, too." Her investments now span various sectors, reflecting her commitment to supporting innovative and diverse business leadership.

Her strategy is highly intentional and deeply personal. Stella looks beyond mere profit, seeking founders and investors that possess, humility, and openness to feedback. She emphasizes the importance of integrity and self-control in entrepreneurs and recognizes the challenges of managing newfound funding responsibly.

Stella's commitment to empowering women in business led her to collaborate with Catherine on *Show Her The Money*. As an associate producer on the film, Stella brings her unique perspective and experiences to the project, helping shed light on women's challenges and triumphs in the investment world. This involvement allows her to amplify the message of gender equity in investing on a broader scale, inspiring more women to enter the field and seek funding for their ventures.

Despite potential financial losses, Stella sees value beyond monetary returns. She emphasizes the knowledge and connections gained through each investment. "I want to combine financial returns with positive social impact while aligning my investments with my personal values. Investing with intention can be both impactful and sustainable," she explains.

As she continues her work as an angel investor and an associate producer of *Show Her The Money*, Stella remains committed to supporting women-led businesses and historically excluded entrepreneurs. Her approach combines financial acumen, deep empathy, and a genuine desire to make a difference. "If you only invest to get financial return, then don't do impact investing," she advises. "You do it because you want to change things."

Stella's story motivates  aspiring investors and entrepreneurs by underscoring the importance of personal conviction, resilience, and the courage to challenge the status quo. As she continues making her mark in angel investing and documentary filmmaking, Stella Lim is a powerful example of how one person's journey can contribute to reshaping entire industries and opening doors for future generations.

### Connect with Stella Lim

# CHAPTER 19

## INSPIRING VISIONARIES

**"WHEN YOU KNOW BETTER, YOU DO BETTER."**
- Maya Angelou


**ANDREA QUINN**
Investor/Associate Producer

In a world where money often speaks louder than words, Andrea Quinn has mastered the art of amplifying women's voices. Part empowerment guru, part savvy investor, she's the secret ingredient in a recipe for women's financial liberation that's been simmering for far too long. With an infectious energy that could power a small city, Andrea has traded the glitz of the fashion photography industry for the grit of transforming how women view their personal and fiscal worth. Her journey is less a career change and more a cosmic calling that reshapes the landscape of women's relationship with money, one emboldened soul at a time.

Growing up in the Bay Area surrounded by a large Hispanic family, Andrea was immersed in an environment of love, support, and female strength from an early age. "I say that my family—all the women, my mother and her sisters, and all of the love and all of the support—I feel like it was my first women's group," Andrea reflects. This foundation of female solidarity, fortified by a father who encouraged her curiosity and pushed her toward greatness, laid the groundwork for Andrea's future as an advocate for women's empowerment.

Her career began in the fast-paced world of fashion, working as a syndication agent for photographers. However, a chance encounter with a client from New York would change the trajectory of her life. "She looked at me and said, 'You know, you should really be a life coach.' And I said, 'What's that?'" Andrea recalls. After reading an article about life coaching, Andrea had an epiphany. "I read that article and was like, 'That's me.' And so, I literally changed my life that day."

Seventeen years later, Andrea has built a thriving coaching practice that seamlessly blends support in life and business. Her client list spans from Wall Street to Hollywood, allowing her to learn from and guide highly influential people across various industries. This unique position has given Andrea invaluable insights into both personal development and business strategy, which she now uses to empower women in their financial journeys. She is an international best-selling author of a book called *The Quinn Essentials* for Women which is based on her popular workshop series where she has taught thousands of women globally.

"What's important to me is that I empower women to get the knowledge they need so that they can make more choices in their lives and use their money—which is their energy, because money is energy," she explains. This philosophy underpins her work as both a coach and an investor.

One of Andrea's most significant contributions to the world of women's empowerment has been investing in and supporting the film, *Show Her The Money*. As a longtime friend and coach to the film's creator, Catherine, Andrea has been involved in the project from its inception. "I feel like I've been here since it was on the ground floor, when it was just a dream," she says.

Andrea's involvement in the film goes beyond mere support. She has been instrumental in bringing investors on board and has invested in the project herself. Her motivation stems from a deep-seated belief in educating women about their financial power. "We only get 2% of all VC money across the board," Andrea notes, highlighting the grim disparity in venture capital.

For Andrea, investing is not just about financial returns but about creating meaningful change. "My best investment is investing in the women who need support and can't afford it," she says. This investment is not just money, it takes many forms—from providing scholarships to her workshops, sending out free books, donating her time, and talking to groups of women about their financial power.

Andrea emphasizes the importance of intuition and alignment with one's values when choosing investments or advising others. "Where do I want my energy to go?" she asks. This approach has led her to invest in many projects like *Show Her The Money*, and most recently, a Broadway-bound production, *Millennials Are Killing Musicals*, also co-produced by Catherine Gray and Debra Smalley— The female-driven story aligns with her mission of empowering women.

Andrea's journey hasn't been without hardships. One of the toughest lessons she's learned is the importance of not holding on too tightly to an idea of how she thinks things should be. "That's the kiss of death in business and investing in life," she reflects. "Holding on too tight prevents any kind of magic from really getting in and expanding things bigger than we could have imagined."

Looking to the future, Andrea is passionate about shifting the conversation around women and money. Her hope for projects like *Show Her The Money* is that they will open eyes and educate people about the realities women face in the business world. "Knowledge is power," she says, "and the more we give knowledge to the masses on every level, we can begin to shift the conversations. You can be angry that we only get 2%, or you can get involved in a conversation about how we really only need 48% more."

Andrea's work serves as a reminder of the ripple effect that can occur when women support and invest in each other. From her books and workshops that inspire women to step into their financial power, to her role in helping to bring *Show Her The Money* to life, Andrea is creating a legacy of empowerment that extends far beyond her individual investments.

She continues to coach, invest, and advocate for women's financial empowerment. Through her work, Andrea endeavors to ensure that more women have the knowledge they need to do better, invest smarter, and ultimately change the landscape of business and finance for future generations.

## Connect with Andrea Quinn

# CHAPTER 20

## CHAMPION OF CHANGE-PAYING IT FORWARD

# "THERE'S A SPECIAL PLACE IN HELL FOR WOMEN WHO DON'T HELP OTHER WOMEN."

- Madeleine Albright

## SHERRY DEUTSCHMANN

Investor/Associate Producer

In a captivating tale of entrepreneurial triumph, Sherry Deutschmann's journey from struggling single mother to formidable angel investor and empowering leader is a profound testament to the transformative power of resilience and unwavering determination. Her story resonates as a personal victory over adversity and a beacon of inspiration for women in the business realm.

Raised in modest circumstances, armed with only a high school diploma, Sherry moved to Nashville to chase dreams of stardom that seemed increasingly out of reach. Her early days were marked by hardships, including times when she couldn't afford electricity, which defined her resolve. "I was a maid, cleaning gas station bathrooms," Sherry reflects. This rough  beginning set the stage for a radical personal and professional revolution.

The pivotal turn in Sherry's life came laced with disparagement and determination. When a former boss belittled her business insights, saying, "You don't know anything about business," Sherry didn't just walk away. "I started my own company right out of my basement, competing with him," she states, her move signaling not just a business decision but a personal rebellion.

Under her leadership, her company, which specialized in the healthcare revenue cycle, thrived by prioritizing employee well-being over conventional corporate metrics. This philosophy wasn't merely idealistic—it was a resounding success, catapulting her business to $40 million in annual revenue, all without accruing debt. Her success culminated in features in *The New York Times* and President Obama's recognition as a White House "Champion of Change," inspiring a new generation of women in business. She went on to distill her experiences and philosophies behind the power of empathy and her employee-first policies in business in her best-selling book, *Lunch With Lucy: Maximize Profits by Investing in Your People.*

After selling her company in 2016, Sherry transitioned into venture capital, focusing on women-owned businesses. Inspired by the barriers she overcame and the systemic obstacles still facing women in business, she says "I became an investor because I wanted to afford more women the opportunity that one investor had done for me." Sherry emphasizes her commitment to fostering a supportive network for women entrepreneurs.

Sherry's venture into angel investing is characterized by a particular focus: supporting determined women entrepreneurs often overlooked by traditional investment avenues. "I don't invest in ideas; I invest in people," she declares, outlining her personal criteria for investment choices. It's about finding women who embody the grit and perseverance she herself demonstrated. Sherry is deeply aware of the systemic biases that often sideline women's business ventures. "The data shows that startups led by women consistently outperform their male counterparts when given equal funding," Sherry points out, highlighting the disconnect between perceptions and reality in venture capital. This drives her to fund women's businesses and advocate for broader changes within the investment community to recognize and rectify these imbalances, emphasizing the urgency of the issue.

In her ongoing investment journey, Sherry has made a troubling yet motivating observation: "Only 2% of women-owned businesses ever get to a million in annual revenue"—a statistic highlighting women's significant barriers and underscoring the vast untapped potential within the business landscape. This insight fuels her mission to mentor and invest in women, aiming to transform these figures and, by extension, the business environment.

Looking to the future, Sherry envisions a venture capital landscape that is far more inclusive and equitable. "The future of venture capital should mirror the diversity of our society," she argues, advocating for a shift in how we make investment decisions. By supporting more women and minorities in entrepreneurship, Sherry believes the entire ecosystem can benefit, leading to more innovation and a healthier economy.

Now 64, an age when many would consider retiring, Sherry has launched BrainTrust, a new venture which is a membership organization for women entrepreneurs, helping them grow and scale their businesses, demonstrating that her mission to empower others is far from over. "I'm working harder than I ever have. It's about helping women grow and scale and witnessing their success," she passionately shares.

Through her investments and personal mentorship, Sherry is changing individual lives and energizing a broader movement toward gender equality in business. Her legacy is defined not only by her success but also by her profound impact on the lives of others. "I build ecosystems of support and success for women," she reflects, her narrative a powerful reminder of how we can all transform personal adversity into a catalyst for widespread change.

## Connect with Sherry Deutschmann

# CHAPTER 21

## LIFTING AND SUPPORTING WOMEN ENTREPRENEURS

**"THERE WILL ALWAYS BE SOMEONE WHO CAN'T SEE YOUR WORTH. DON'T LET IT BE YOU."**

- Mel Robbins

**CARRIE MURRAY**

Investor/Associate Producer

Carrie Murray is leading a quiet revolution in the heart of Los Angeles. As the founder of the BRA Network (Business Relationship Alliance), she's creating spaces for women and non-binary entrepreneurs to thrive, support each other, and tackle one of the most persistent taboos in business: money.

Her path to championing women in entrepreneurship and investing was as unpredictable as it was transformative. Her story begins on the island of Guam, where she was born into the nomadic life of a military family. Every three years brought a new home, a new school, and the challenge of forging new friendships. This constant upheaval cultivated in Carrie a remarkable adaptability—a skill that would serve her well in her future endeavors. But it was her mother who first showed Carrie what it meant to break the mold.

"My mom was one of the only moms that worked," Carrie recalls. "She started as a secretary, eventually moved up in ranks, and went to college as an adult. We actually took a math class together because we were in college at the same time."

As the first person in her family to graduate college, Carrie initially pursued a career in social work, focusing on domestic violence prevention. However, after two years as a court advocate in the San Francisco DA's office, she found the work emotionally draining and decided to change course.

A series of career pivots followed—from aspiring actor to public school teacher and principal. But her leap into entrepreneurship would set her on the path to founding BRA. After leaving her role as a principal, Carrie started a school for twice-exceptional children and gifted students who also have a learning or developmental disability, but quickly realized she lacked the business acumen to make it successful. "I could teach and run a school, but not a business," Carrie admits. "I was failing at it, so I had to seek support."

Her search for guidance led her to networking events, which she found dominated by mostly older white men who seemed indifferent to her presence. Feeling frustrated and out of place, "I just kept thinking, 'Where are all the women?'" Carrie remembers. "Where are the women business owners?"

Undeterred by the lack of support, Carrie took matters into her own hands. She began hosting dinner parties in her backyard, inviting fellow women entrepreneurs—an accountant, a photographer, an event designer, and a hairstylist. These intimate gatherings quickly outgrew her space as word spread. What started as casual conversations over home-cooked meals and bottles of wine evolved into the BRA Network, officially launching in 2017. From those first five members sharing their struggles and triumphs, BRA has blossomed into a thriving community of nearly 500 highly engaged members nationwide and beyond, extending as far as Canada and Norway.

BRA's mission goes beyond simple networking. It's about creating a supportive ecosystem where women hire each other, collaborate on projects and, importantly, break the silence surrounding financial matters. "One of the things that kept coming up in our meetings and networking was money, pricing, and scaling," Carrie explains. It was always a taboo topic. "When women would get together to talk about what they charge, they really struggled with talking openly about it."

This realization motivated Carrie to expand her efforts. She launched a podcast called "Get Carried Away," where she interviews women who can answer pressing questions about money, pricing, and financial strategies.

Carrie also established the Wealthy Women's Summit, a two-day conference designed as a space where women can openly ask uncomfortable questions about money. The summit aims to create an environment where attendees can discuss pricing strategies, learn how to properly charge what they're worth, and explore topics like investing. Carrie invites prominent women in finance, such as Catherine Gray, Arlan Hamilton, and Rachel Rogers, to participate in fireside chats, providing expert insights on these crucial financial matters. These discussions cover various topics, from overcoming money blocks to understanding what funders look for in potential investments.

It was at one of these summits that the seeds for *Show Her The Money* were planted. The event featured a panel called "Girls Just Wanna Have Funds," which included Catherine Gray and other fund owners focused on funding for women entrepreneurs. That panel became a springboard for connections that would later shape the documentary. Here, Catherine met Kelly Ann Winget, who later became an investor in the film, and was introduced to Dapper Boi, a brand featured in the documentary, as an example of a struggling business with a compelling story and unique product.

For Carrie, investing in *Show Her The Money* was a natural extension of her mission. "It's very meta, right?" she laughs. "You're investing in something that's talking about investing." The film's focus on getting more money into the hands of those historically underrepresented resonated deeply with Carrie, who had been a guest twice on Catherine's podcast "Invest in Her," discussing this very topic. The statistics were stark: Black-owned women's businesses receive less than 0.01% of venture funding, and the overall rate for women-owned businesses has been stuck at 2% for decades. Carrie saw the film as an opportunity to raise awareness and move the needle on these persistent inequities.

As Carrie delved deeper into the investing world, a realization shattered her preconceptions. "I realized, oh, you don't need millions," she explains, her voice carrying a hint of excitement. "What if instead you got five friends who could each get $10,000 to invest in a year? Well, now we have $50,000 to invest in something." This collaborative approach to investing aligns perfectly with Carrie's philosophy of supporting and elevating women-owned businesses. She sees it as a way to address women entrepreneurs' persistent funding gap, embodying the spirit of the old adage, 'a rising tide lifts all boats.'

"Knowing what I know now, I would have started so much sooner," she admits. Her advice to young people emphasizes early action and attentiveness: Start with small, consistent savings and stay alert to financial opportunities and changing interest rates. When guiding aspiring women investors, Carrie champions authenticity and enthusiasm. She challenges them to examine their own interests and motivations: "What are you passionate about? What gets you fired up?" she asks. "Find people trying to come up with a solution to things that charge you up, that get you excited, that get you motivated."

Carrie emphasizes what she looks for in founders to invest in: "I really want to know what problem they're solving and how they're solving it. I look for innovation and creativity. And I definitely look for, 'Has anybody looked at this problem this way?'"

Throughout Carrie's journey, from her early career aspirations to her current role as a community builder and investor, she's carried a piece of wisdom from her father. When she expressed interest in becoming a flight attendant as a child, he told her, "Don't be the stewardess; be the pilot." This simple yet powerful advice has become a guiding principle, pushing her to aim higher and take charge in her professional life.

Today, as she continues to grow the BRA Network and explore new investment opportunities, Carrie sees herself as part of a larger movement. "We are literally at the beginning of a renaissance," she declares, referring to the increasing economic power of women and the potential for transformative change in the business world.

For Carrie Murray, empowering women through community, education, and investment isn't just a career—it's a mission. As she continues to break down barriers and create opportunities for women entrepreneurs, she's helping to shape a more equitable future in business and finance.

### Connect with Carrie Murray

# CHAPTER 22

# INVESTING IN FOUNDERS WITH STRENGTH AND PERSEVERANCE

**"NEVER DOUBT THAT A SMALL GROUP OF THOUGHTFUL, COMMITTED CITIZENS CAN CHANGE THE WORLD; INDEED, IT'S THE ONLY THING THAT EVER HAS."**

- Margaret Mead

**HELEN FANUCCI**

Investor/Associate Producer

In the dynamic world of venture capital, Helen Fanucci is a committed leader advocating for women's entrepreneurial success. Her journey—from a childhood marked by activism and early loss to a trailblazing career in tech—has led her to found businesses of her own and to promote funding for other women entrepreneurs.

Born in upstate New York, Helen was raised in a family where activism was both modeled and expected. Her father marched with Dr. Martin Luther King Jr. in Alabama and Helen joined her mother on the Boston Commons following Roe v. Wade, experiencing firsthand how the power of even small groups of committed women can change the whole world.

From a young age, Helen was outspoken and exhibited strong leadership qualities, often organizing and captaining her kickball team. A sixth-grade teacher's comment about her "tendency to influence other kids" filled her with pride and validated her drive and ability to shape her world. At 13 when Helen's mother passed away, her commitment to self-reliance took deeper root. Determined to chart her own path, she set her sights on MIT, where she studied mechanical engineering and developed skills that would fuel her career in tech over four high-impact decades.

In the early 1980s, Helen began her professional career in Silicon Valley, joining IBM as a manufacturing engineer and later moving into sales, where she sold IBM's hardware and software to the booming tech industry. Through these experiences, she became acutely aware of the venture capital world's role in driving innovation and creating opportunities. Throughout her career, Helen frequently observed gender bias in action, often seeing men promoted over more qualified women.

A key shift in her career occurred when a conversation with a former Microsoft customer opened her eyes to the disparity of venture capital funding for women. As an investor and associate producer on Catherine Gray's film *Show Her The Money*, Helen was deeply drawn to the mission of bridging the funding gap for women. "I knew I had to be part of this," she says. "The film connected me with a community of women founders, VCs, and limited partners who share this mission."

Realizing she could do more than advocate, Helen began investing directly in women entrepreneurs. "I realized I could have even more impact by putting my money where my mouth is and investing in these businesses," she recalls. As a limited partner in SoGal Ventures, Emmeline Ventures, and Swizzle Ventures, and an angel investor in Dapper Boi, Helen continues to focus on closing the female funding divide and supporting the growth of early-stage women-founded businesses.

"I invest in people," she says, describing her admiration for founders who show tenacity and fortitude. Helen is driven to not only fund women's ventures but also to push for systemic change within the investment community. "Data shows that startups led by women, even when supplied with inferior funding, routinely outperform those led by men," she notes, clearly expressing her belief in the untapped potential of women entrepreneurs to build robust businesses that deliver outsized financial returns.

For aspiring investors, Helen emphasizes finding mentors and networks that can guide early investments. "Take a first step—find people and funds that help you put a toe in the water," she advises. Her vision for the future is a venture capital landscape that optimizes opportunity for investors and entrepreneurs while reflecting the realities of our diverse society.

Helen is also the best-selling author of *Love Your Team: A Survival Guide for Sales Managers in a Hybrid World.* Over her 25-year career on the front lines at top tech companies including Apple, Sun Microsystems, IBM, and Microsoft, she developed the *Love Your Team* system of management. Inspired by the women founders she has met, Helen also co-founded PipelinePower.AI, where she now serves as CEO, helping organizations accelerate revenue growth and deliver on their promise to founders, investors, and customers.

Outside of her professional life, Helen enjoys and supports musical theater, a passion that has stayed with her since childhood. She also stays active with regular pickleball games, traveling the world, and spending time with family and friends.

As an early activist for women's rights who built a successful career in the male-dominated tech world, Helen Fanucci is committed to positively impacting women founders and their investors while driving progress toward gender equity in business and entrepreneurship. She firmly believes in the power of individuals to make a difference.

### Connect with Helen Fanucci

# CHAPTER 23

# BLAZING TRAILS WITH INVESTMENTS IN DIVERSE FOUNDERS

**"IF WE HAVE DATA, LET'S LOOK AT DATA. IF ALL WE HAVE ARE OPINIONS, LET'S GO WITH MINE."**

- Jim Barksdale

# LORENZO THIONE

Investor/Associate Producer

In a world where specialization is often the key to success, Lorenzo Thione stands out as a Renaissance man for the digital age. With a career spanning from artificial intelligence to Broadway production, Thione's journey defies conventional narratives of investment success.

As a child growing up in Milan, while his peers dreamed of soccer stardom, young Lorenzo had a peculiar bedtime routine. "From a very young age, like seven or eight, instead of asking my mom to read me a good night story, I would ask her to teach me the foundations of BASIC programming," he chuckles.

His early fascination with code set the stage for a life that would weave together seemingly disparate threads: computer engineering, entrepreneurship, venture capital, and, eventually, the glittering world of Broadway theater. Lorenzo's story is not just one of professional success but of personal transformation and a commitment to backing diversity in the often homogenous tech investment world.

Growing up, Lorenzo faced the difficulties of coming to terms with his identity as a gay man in a society that wasn't always accepting. He channeled his energy into his studies, excelling in computer engineering. It wasn't until he moved to the United States at age 21 to pursue graduate studies at the University of Texas at Austin that he found the courage to come out.

The move to America marked a significant turning point in Lorenzo's life, both personally and professionally. "I arrived only a few months before September 11th happened," he recalls. "That was an impactful moment for me." The tragedy prompted Lorenzo to live more authentically, leading to his decision to come out publicly. It also gave him a taste of the uncertainty faced by immigrants in America, an experience that would later influence his career choices.

Lorenzo's professional journey began at FX Pal, a subsidiary of Xerox PARC, where he worked on natural language processing—a field that would later explode with the advent of AI technologies like ChatGPT. In 2003, he co-founded his first company, one of the earliest artificial intelligence semantic web search companies. This venture provided a crash course in entrepreneurship and venture capital, culminating in a successful sale to Microsoft in 2008.

The sale marked another pivotal moment in Lorenzo's career. Rather than resting on his laurels, he saw an opportunity to support others like himself. "I saw a gap in the world regarding supporting LGBTQ entrepreneurs," Lorenzo explains. This realization led him to found StartOut, which remains the largest entrepreneurship organization for the LGBTQ community.

Lorenzo's journey took a surprising turn when his passion for language and storytelling led him to Broadway. He co-wrote and produced *Allegiance*, a musical about the internment of Japanese Americans, featuring George Takei. This success launched a prolific career as a Broadway producer, earning him four Tony nominations and two Tony Awards. "Right now, I'm actively an investor and a producer. I have four shows on Broadway this year and am working on three more for the future."

Despite his success in entertainment, Lorenzo has always maintained his connection to the tech industry. He continued to invest as an angel investor, learning valuable lessons along the way. "My worst decision about passing on any investment was Uber," Lorenzo admits with a laugh. "But I don't regret it. That was the only decision I could make at the time with the information I had."

Today, Lorenzo is a managing partner at Gaingels, focusing on making the venture capital world as diverse and representative as possible. "We are investors in a couple of the companies featured in *Show Her The Money*," Lorenzo notes. "Which is not to say that that's the reason I'm involved with the film. I think, actually, it's the other way around. Catherine got connected to Gaingels as part of her and I meeting to, amongst other things, start working on this project together."

Gaingels' mission agrees perfectly with Lorenzo's personal ideology. "If you're leaving half of the population effectively to fend for itself, and you have little to no allies or supporters from the group that holds the most power, from the group that holds the most access, from the group that controls the most capital, then you make it all the more difficult for that parity, for that equality to sort of be achieved," he explains.

Lorenzo's approach to investing is as unique as his background. He looks for businesses that excite him, whether health and fitness companies like Whoop and Oura or innovative media ventures like Pocket Pod, which creates personalized AI-generated podcasts. "I look for things that I get excited about. That I would use or that I understand," he says. "I invest in people that I think are exceptional. If I meet you and you strike me as someone with incredible drive and agency—not waiting for things to happen to you but going out in the world and making it happen—and you're trying to solve a big enough problem, chances are, I'm going to be interested."

But beyond personal interest, Lorenzo is driven by a desire to make a difference. He has, for instance, invested in companies working on cures for HIV, seeing poetic justice in supporting solutions to a disease that once devastated the LGBTQ community.

For founders seeking investment, Lorenzo offers pragmatic advice. "Think about it as a sales process," he suggests. "Build a CRM (customer relationship management) and speak to hundreds of investors. Build a pipeline and cultivate it." He emphasizes the importance of warm introductions and networking, urging founders to build relationships with investors even before they need funding. "But ultimately", he says, "be prepared to tell a story—one that moves, entertains and inspires. That's how you close the deal."

Lorenzo's journey from a curious child in Milan to a Broadway producer is a stunning example of the power of following one's passions and using success to create opportunities for others. His story embodies the essence of the American dream while highlighting the work still to be done to make that dream accessible to all. As he continues to invest in groundbreaking companies and produce award-winning shows, Lorenzo Thione remains committed to measurably impacting diversity and inclusion in tech and venture capital.

## Connect with Lorenzo Thione

# WOMEN-LED COMPANIES ARE DIRECTLY RESPONSIBLE FOR 23 MILLION JOBS.

Source: World Bank Group

# CHAPTER 24

# DOING GOOD BY
# DOING WELL

# "IF WE WANT TO SEE CHANGE IN THE WORLD, WE NEED TO CREATE IT, INVEST IN IT, AND BE IT!"

- Marcia Dawood

## MARCIA DAWOOD

Investor/Associate Producer

As an angel investor, author, and advisor to the Securities and Exchange Commission, Marcia Dawood is reshaping the venture capital landscape with a laser focus on supporting women-led businesses and historically excluded entrepreneurs. Her journey from corporate America to the forefront of angel investing exemplifies how personal experiences and a keen awareness of systemic barriers can drive meaningful change in the business world.

Marcia's story begins in a small town outside Reading, Pennsylvania, where she grew up as an only child in a stable, middle-class family. Her father, a meticulous budgeter, instilled in her an early appreciation for financial management. "My dad used to show me the budget and would go over it with me when I was pretty young," Marcia recalls. This early exposure to financial concepts would later prove instrumental in her trajectory.

After college, Marcia embarked on a career in corporate America, spending over sixteen years with the same company. However, a chance invitation to an angel investing meeting in 2012 would drastically alter her professional path. "I had no idea what angel investing was," Marcia admits. Accompanying her husband to a local gathering in Pittsburgh, the meeting opened Marcia's eyes to a world of possibilities beyond her corporate role. "I was totally fascinated by the innovation around me," she explains.

This newfound passion for entrepreneurship and investment coincided with a series of moves driven by her husband's career. Over the next decade, Marcia and her husband relocated eight times, living in diverse cities, including Pittsburgh, New York City, Dallas, San Francisco, and Charlotte. "It gave me a really interesting perspective of the ecosystem within these different places," she reflects on this whirlwind period. These moves, though challenging, provided Marcia with unique insights into the varying challenges and opportunities faced by entrepreneurs and investors across different regions of America.

As Marcia became more involved in the world of angel investing, she noticed a troubling disconnect. Despite the potential for individuals to make a significant impact through early-stage investments, many people were not aware of this opportunity. "I would talk to people and feel that investing in early-stage companies is so foreign to them, they have no idea they can participate," she explains.

Driven by her realization, Marcia embarked on a mission to demystify angel investing and make it accessible to a broader audience. As she evolved from novice to expert, she took on pivotal roles in the industry. She became Chair of the Board for the Angel Capital Association and later secured a position as an advisor to the Securities and Exchange Commission for small business capital formation.

With a intense focus on empowering the underrepresented, Marcia's approach to investing transcends traditional financial metrics. Her commitment to inclusivity is evident. By recognizing inherent barriers, Marcia has made it her mission to level the playing field. "If we could get more women and more people of color to be investors, then we're going to get more funding to women and people of color," she explains. Her goal goes beyond financial returns, focusing on creating systemic change and opening doors for underrepresented founders in the venture capital landscape.

One of the critical lessons Marcia learned along the way was the importance of diversification through angel funds. "Venture funds were like gold to me," she explains, "because I can put in a little bit of money and I can get access to 8, 10, 12, 15 companies simultaneously." Her approach not only mitigates risk but also makes angel investing more accessible to those who may not have large sums to invest in individual companies.

Marcia also candidly shares moments of doubt, including a period in early 2020 when she questioned the viability of this path. "I don't know about this angel investing thing. This seems crazy," she remembers thinking. However, a series of successful exits later that year reinvigorated her enthusiasm and confirmed the potential of patient, strategic investing.

Drawing from these experiences, Marcia identified a crucial resource gap for aspiring angel investors—a roadmap for getting started. Her realization led her to write her book, *Doing Good While Doing Well: Invest for Change, Reap Financial Rewards, and Increase Your Happiness*. The book aims to provide a comprehensive guide for those interested in angel investing, covering everything from the basics to more advanced strategies.

"I'm trying to give people a few exercises, worksheets, all the things I wish I had when I started," Marcia explains. Her goal is to show readers that angel investing is doable and accessible, even for those who may feel intimidated by the financial world.

In her book, Marcia introduces a crucial concept, the "halo strategy," her take on what venture capitalists call an investment thesis. The framework helps angel investors define their priorities, set boundaries, and make more informed decisions.

Marcia's insights extend beyond individual investing strategies. She strongly advocates for policy changes that could make angel investing more inclusive. Reflecting on her role as an SEC advisor, she questions the current accredited investor definition, which relies heavily on income and wealth metrics. "How about we just educate people and let them know about the risks?" she suggests, emphasizing the need for more comprehensive investor education rather than relying solely on financial thresholds.

Marcia has remained committed to supporting women-led businesses and historically excluded entrepreneurs throughout her journey. She shares the story of one of her most successful investments, Joylux, which develops products for women's health issues. The company's resilience during the COVID-19 pandemic and its innovative approach to growth exemplify the kind of visionary leadership Marcia seeks in her investments.

Looking to the future, Marcia is optimistic about the potential for angel investing to drive meaningful change in the entrepreneurial landscape. "If you can't be an investor, don't just sit on the sidelines of this problem," Marcia advises. "You can still do something really impactful with how you spend, where you bank, and how you use your time." Through her work, writing, and mentorship, Marcia Dawood is opening doors and creating opportunities for the next generation of entrepreneurs and investors, proving that doing good and doing well can indeed go hand in hand.

### Connect with Marcia Dawood

# CHAPTER 25

# THE POWER OF ANGEL INVESTING

**"DO NOT FOLLOW WHERE THE PATH MAY LEAD. GO INSTEAD WHERE THERE IS NO PATH AND LEAVE A TRAIL."**

- Muriel Strode

## SUE BEVAN BAGGOTT

Investor/Associate Producer

"If you had told me even 10 years ago that I would be doing this work, I would have laughed at you," Sue Bevan Baggott admits with a chuckle. Sue's experience with angel investing is a testament to the enduring power of family values and the unexpected paths life can take. Growing up in a family that valued helping others, but had limited financial resources, she learned the power of service, but never imagined she'd one day become an early-stage angel and venture capital investor.

Despite their tight budget, her family always found ways to contribute, prioritizing the giving of time and labor over monetary donations. This mindset manifested in various ways, from volunteering at their church to Sue's decision, at just seven or eight years old, to learn sign language to communicate with deaf children at a local school. Her family culture of giving back was complemented by a strong emphasis on education. Sue also learned about pushing boundaries, not letting her small stature and childhood asthma discourage her from playing sports "like the boys did."

Sue's grandfather constantly reinforced the importance of using one's talents for the greater good. His advice to "use your talents to the fullest in service of others" became a guiding principle in Sue's life, shaping her future decisions and career path in ways she couldn't have anticipated as a child.

He also recognized her aptitude for science and math, and encouraged her to become an engineer, despite how male-dominated the field was in the 1980's. He told her, "Engineers learn to solve big problems and make the world a better place." His words inspired Sue to pursue engineering, equipping her with the drive to innovate and leave an indelible mark.

Sue studied engineering at Lehigh University, attending classes where only one in ten students was female. After graduating, Sue began her career in global innovation at Procter & Gamble. There, she honed her skills in developing breakthrough products to improve consumers' everyday lives, working on megabrands from Pantene to Pampers. As her career progressed and her financial situation improved, Sue's approach to giving back evolved from volunteering to donating to nonprofits and serving on boards.

"I joke that I am an accidental angel investor," Sue says, reflecting on her unexpected journey. This "accident" would prove to be a turning point, allowing Sue to combine her family's values of giving back, her professional expertise in innovation, and her passion for creating positive change in a way she never anticipated. It's a route that not only transformed Sue's own life but has since impacted countless entrepreneurs and communities, proving that the seeds of service planted in childhood can blossom in the most unexpected and powerful ways.

In 2014, while leading a strategy project for a University of Cincinnati board focused on collaboration between the university, large companies, and community members, she met Tony Shipley. Tony was a successful entrepreneur who had created an angel investing group after selling his company. Sue was initially skeptical of angel investing, seeing it as a domain dominated by older, wealthy men solely focused on financial returns. However, Tony's approach was different. He believed in diversifying the group to make better investment decisions and support a broader range of entrepreneurs.

Tony recognized Sue's strategic thinking skills and hired her to lead a strategy refresh for his group, Queen City Angels (QCA). Despite her lack of experience in angel investing, Sue brought fresh insights through stakeholder interviews with group members, and partners.

He invited Sue to join QCA, and connected her with a national effort to train more women in the field. "I went from zero involvement in angel investing in 2015 to joining QCA, plus Senior Kaufman Fellow Alicia Robb's pilot fund, and her Next Wave Impact Fund investment committee by the end of 2016," Sue recalls.

As she delved deeper into the world of angel investing, Sue identified four main barriers preventing people, especially women, from getting involved: awareness of the asset class, education on the process, risk astuteness, and respect within the early-stage investing community (historically dominated by men). Determined to address these barriers, Sue and her husband created the QCA Ascent program, providing an accessible entry point for new early-stage investors.

"We ended up more than tripling the size of Queen City Angels in five years by putting our starter tier program in place," Sue says proudly. "We now have over 200 investors from across the US, including many more young investors, women, and people of color."

For Sue, angel investing isn't just about financial returns—it's about driving positive change in the world. She looks for founders with strong leadership skills, the ability to build relationships, and a clear sense of purpose. "I want to see that the company is going to make a positive difference in the world," she explains. "That can be job growth in a region, a healthcare innovation that's going to save lives...I choose to define positive impact broadly."

Sue is intensely passionate about investing in diverse founding teams, drawing on her experience in global innovation at P&G. "We delivered the most transformative innovations when we had people from around the world working together," she reflects. This belief drives her to seek out and support various entrepreneurs who might be overlooked by traditional investment avenues.

One of Sue's proudest investments is in the Next Wave Impact Fund, which she says "disproves the theory that you can't have purpose and profitability and high growth all together." This fund focuses on purpose-driven companies demonstrating that profit and purpose can indeed go hand in hand.

Upon reflection, Sue wishes she had discovered angel investing earlier in her career. "I wish I had understood how much innovation was happening, and all the ways I could help advance more female entrepreneurs."

Today, Sue wears many hats: innovation consultant, investor, advisor, and board member. She's driven by the belief that investing is a powerful tool for shaping the future. "As women, we are socialized to save money or give it away. We are not socialized to be investors," Sue observes. "And yet there is so much power in investing to change the direction of innovation, to solve today's biggest problems, and to shape who the future leaders are."

From a child determined to prove girls could do anything, to a successful early-stage investor Sue embodies the power of resilience, determination, and a commitment to making a difference.

"Each one of us, in our own way, can accelerate change," she affirms. "It just requires a little courage to take those first steps."

## Connect with Sue Bevan Baggott

# CHAPTER 26

# CORPORATE WOMEN BEING CHAMPIONS OF ANGEL INVESTING

**"LIFT AS YOU RISE."**

- Bonang Mohale

# JOANNE TAYLOR

Investor/Associate Producer

In the high-powered world of corporate transformation, Joanne Taylor is a force to be reckoned with. As an advisor at AlixPartners and co-lead of a global transformation practice, she deftly navigates the intricate maze of corporate restructuring and private equity with the precision of a seasoned strategist. But Joanne's bold leap into angel investing truly sets her apart, igniting a passion that has been simmering throughout her career.

Joanne's story begins in the suburbs of Los Angeles where, as a young girl, she found herself an unlikely apprentice in her father's wholesale automotive supply  business. "I don't know how he did this, but he took me everywhere," Joanne recalls. From accompanying him on sales calls to implementing warehouse management systems at the tender age of 13, these early experiences laid the foundation for Joanne's business acumen and innate ability to assess situations rapidly.

But it wasn't just her father who shaped her worldview. Joanne's mother was crucial in exposing her to strong, daring women. "My mother made sure that I could witness strong women and women that may have taken, you know, let's call it pioneering paths," Joanne explains. She remembers attending an AAUW (American Association of University Women) summit for young women in high school where she saw astronauts and business executives, opening her eyes to a world of possibilities.

When her father's business failed during her high school years, it left an indelible mark on Joanne. "It was pretty traumatic for me when it happened," she says. Her immediate reaction was to avoid business entirely, stating, "I vowed never to go into it," but the experience ultimately refined her financial instincts and sensitized her to the human aspects of commerce.

Despite her initial reluctance, Joanne was led back to the business world. "I got my MBA and went into consulting," she explains. This decision marked a turning point, allowing her to leverage her innate talents in a new context. Her entry into consulting, specifically in global systems integration work, provided a platform for Joanne to apply her expertise in a broader, more stable environment than her father's entrepreneurial venture.

As Joanne's career flourished, she became increasingly aware of the disparities women faced in leadership roles. "What I noticed over many years of doing that work was the very different introduction for women than men as leaders," she reflects. Her observation and a growing recognition of her privilege ignited a profound shift in Joanne's professional focus.

Joanne's journey into angel investing began with self-reflection and personal growth. "I had some events in my life that I needed help getting through and figuring out what was next," she shares, which led her to seek coaching from Andrea Quinn.

When Andrea presented Joanne with the opportunity to invest in *Show Her The Money*, Joanne responded immediately and enthusiastically. "She told me what the film was about and I said, 'I'll give you whatever you ask for,'" she recalls telling Andrea. "It just feels right."

More than just a financial investment, this decision represented a commitment to a cause that resonated deeply with Joanne's values. "I'm really passionate about elevating women holistically," she explains. Her involvement with the film project opened her eyes to the power of targeted investment in women-led businesses and the potential for creating systemic change.

Joanne's approach to investing defies convention. While her day job involves working with global private equity giants, her personal investment philosophy stems from a desire for congruity between profits and core values. "We need to elevate our consciousness and realize that we are all connected and should consider a philosophy of 'a high tide lifts all boats'," she asserts.

Her commitment to empowerment extends beyond angel investing. Through her involvement with Outreach International, a nonprofit focused on eliminating systemic poverty, Joanne has witnessed firsthand the transformative power of community-focused development. She sees her international development work and angel investing as catalysts for widespread social change, emphasizing how empowering women entrepreneurs can transform entire communities.

As Joanne continues to navigate her path in angel investing and define her investment thesis, she focuses on identifying opportunities that promise financial returns, align with her values, and have the potential for generational impact.

Looking ahead, Joanne sees *Show Her The Money* as a catalyst for change in investing and broader societal attitudes towards women in business. "My hope for this film is that it builds awareness around the intentional exclusion of women," she states. More importantly, she believes the film will inspire action. "The change will happen on the backs of women."

The latest chapter in Joanne's professional journey isn't just about diversifying her portfolio. It's a declaration of her unwavering commitment to empowering women and reshaping the financial landscape. With each investment, Joanne isn't just backing businesses; she's fueling a revolution in how we think about power, capital, and female leadership in the 21st century.

### Connect with Joanne Taylor

# CHAPTER 27

# WEALTH BUILDING THROUGH ENTREPRENEURSHIP

# "BELIEVE IN THE POWER OF POSSIBILITY."

- Dr. Henry Johnson

## JILL JOHNSON

Investor/Associate Producer

Jill Johnson's childhood home was a hub of entrepreneurial energy and social consciousness. From a young age, Jill absorbed lessons about business ownership through a community impact lens as her parents' newspaper publishing business supported community events and provided a first opportunity to many young journalists. From cash flow to hiring to customer service, Jill's front-row seat to entrepreneurship set the stage for the work she does today.

One of the publications in the portfolio was the Minority Business Journal, which was the foundation of Jill's understanding of the barriers that Black business owners face. "Back when they had their publications, access to capital was an ongoing conversation, so I've been hearing about this problem since high school," Jill recalls. This early exposure to the roadblocks faced by minority-owned businesses was a constant backdrop to her upbringing. "I was not the easiest child to raise," she chuckles. "I was always the kid who asked, 'Well, why not? Why can't I do that?'" This curious spirit and her father's mantra to "believe in the power of possibility" drove Jill to question the status quo and shaped her approach to problem-solving and innovation.

Little did Jill know that the dinner table conversations about access to capital for historically excluded business owners would become the soundtrack of her career. These early exposures to the barriers to business success laid the foundation for a lifelong commitment of creating more opportunities for others.

From Harvard to Goldman Sachs, Jill's journey took an illuminating turn. Her three years in investment banking opened her eyes to a world vastly different from her parents' business experience. "It was a whole different side of the coin where access to capital and resources was not a challenge," Jill says, reflecting on her time in the Goldman Sachs Investment Banking Financial Analyst Program. "I was exposed to entrepreneurs who were selling companies they started for a lot of money, whereas my parents talked about passing the business down to the kids."

This contrast was especially poignant when her parents, wanting to retire, shut down the business after 20 years without a succession or exit plan. "It was such a tremendous loss," Jill recalls, "because while it provided a good lifestyle for us growing up, the business wasn't used to create wealth within the family through an exit." This moment crystallized a crucial distinction for Jill: the contrast between creating a legacy through a business itself and generating wealth through it. "Many people think selling a business has to be a tech company that gets acquired or a large company that is sold to another large company," she notes, "but there are dry cleaning businesses, accounting businesses, and even food truck businesses being bought and sold every day." This realization jump-started Jill's enthusiasm for wealth-building through entrepreneurship.

Armed with these insights and driven by a lifelong commitment to community impact, Jill took action. In the early 2000s, she and her father conceived a bold plan: raising a fund to address the persistent capital gap for historically excluded populations. Their enthusiasm for a solution to directly address the problem was met with resistance. "We continued to be told that we wouldn't be able to raise capital due to our lack of fund management experience," Jill recalls. "And, we continued to hear that capital was plentiful, however, the business owners needed more training to be capital ready." This feedback, while frustrating, would ultimately shape the next phase of Jill's journey.

In 2002, Jill and her father founded the Institute for Entrepreneurial Leadership (IFEL) to respond to the perceived need for entrepreneurial education for business owners in the Newark area. They started with a $25,000 planning grant and five clients. Jill and her father worked tirelessly to provide the high-touch support that business owners needed to overcome the barriers to success. Jill became the organization's CEO in 2011.

In 2018, Jill experienced a jarring revelation after reviewing old IFEL proposals during an office cleanout. Despite nearly two decades of work, exponential growth in the number of small business training programs, and the proliferation of online information, the needle had barely moved on capital access for Black entrepreneurs.

"Okay, wait a second," Jill thought to herself. "Training and education for these entrepreneurs has not led to more capital so we need to look in a different direction for solutions. We're going to tackle this issue at a systemic level because that's the only way to create real change." Energized by the revelation, Jill pivoted IFEL's focus to address the root causes of unequal access to capital.

She set her sights on dispelling the notion that capital finds the best entrepreneurs with the best businesses. Jill is very clear in her belief that capital finds its way to companies led by entrepreneurs who are connected to people who control the capital. "Ability to access capital is directly proportional to an entrepreneur's connectivity to people with money," Jill says. "People invest in people who they know, like, and trust. Relationships with people who have money create a more direct pathway to capital."

This pivot led IFEL to launch several initiatives to increase diversity in the investor community. One such initiative, "The Making of Black Angels," focuses on raising awareness about angel investing within the Black community. The success of this program deepened IFEL's involvement within the investor ecosystem and eventually led to IFEL's acquisition of Pipeline Angels, an angel investor training program and network committed to changing the face of angel investing.

Jill said, "We chose angel investing because people can invest their own money however they'd like. We train people to invest in the people and the causes that they care about, and we help them understand that they have the power to change the access to capital status quo." Her involvement with *Show Her The Money* aligns precisely with her mission. "It's telling the story in a powerful way that can foster a mindset shift about why women receive less capital," Jill explains. "That's the first step toward systemic change."

However, Jill also stresses the importance of addressing intersectionality in conversations about women in entrepreneurship and investing. "When we say 'all women,' it usually ends up meaning white women," she notes, recognizing the compounded challenges faced by women of color in the entrepreneurial space.

IFEL's sponsorship of *Show Her The Money* is part of a larger strategy to foster "conscious collisions" between investors and entrepreneurs outside their regular network. Through IFEL's Creating Conscious events, Jill facilitates connections that would never happen organically, challenging attendees to open doors for amazing women innovators who have had difficulty raising significant amounts of capital.

"While biases and discrimination affect many groups within our population, historical exclusion from wealth-building was more targeted and was enforced through laws and policies," Jill explains. "To unpack all the issues, we have to address and incorporate the issues experienced by each group and identify solutions for each group separately. In so doing, we create systems that work for everyone."

Today, through IFEL and the support of initiatives like *Show Her The Money*, Jill continues the work that her parents began with the Minority Business Journal and their other ventures. She's committed to creating a world where more people have an opportunity for entrepreneurial success.

Looking ahead, Jill remains focused on the vision she and her father shared—removing barriers to wealth-building through entrepreneurship. "In 20 years, we just shouldn't be having these same conversations about access to capital for specific groups of entrepreneurs," she asserts. Her journey, deeply influenced by her parents' path and through experiences in resource-rich circles, serves as a powerful reminder of the long-standing, deep-seated nature of these challenges and the need for systemic change.

### Connect with Jill Johnson

# CHAPTER 28

# INSPIRING CHANGE IN FINANCE AND INVESTING

**"SHE REMEMBERED WHO SHE WAS, AND THE GAME CHANGED. SHE REMEMBERED WHO SHE WAS, AND THE POWER CHANGED."**

- Lalah Delia

## MARY ROSE

Investor/Associate Producer

Mary Rose's journey in finance is a compelling blend of personal growth and professional evolution. From her early days in Ann Arbor, Michigan to her current role in private credit, Mary's path was shaped by a desire to merge financial success with meaningful contribution.

Raised by loving parents who emphasized education as the pathway to success, Mary recalls, "I never had any element of, 'You can't do this because of your gender.'" It was a supportive environment that laid the foundation for her future. She cites third grade as a pivotal moment when she received the math champion trophy, an early recognition of her aptitude that would later influence her career choices. "As funny as it seems, that was really meaningful to me."

After a childhood influenced by parents who committed their whole lives to helping others, Mary faced an internal conflict when she entered the workforce. "I struggled with how to marry that blend of giving back with really feeling very strongly about being financially independent," she explains. This dichotomy between her parents' model of selfless giving and her desire for financial independence would shape her future decisions.

Mary's career in finance began to take shape, eventually leading her to Antares Capital, a global alternative asset manager. Over 25 years in the private credit arena, she achieved career success in an industry where women in senior roles are scarce. During this time, Mary had a crucial realization: She didn't have to leave finance to make a difference. "I finally realized that the biggest impact I was going to have was actually staying with the industry I had built my career in and harnessing that influence here," she says.

This epiphany set the stage for Mary's personal journey into angel investing, which began about four years ago. "I had just gone through a divorce, and I felt very grateful for having the ability to financially support myself through that transition." She reminisces, "I wanted to have the ability to give back to others so that they can achieve the same level of empowerment."

What began as a personal reflection quickly became a strategic approach to creating impact. Starting with small angel investments, she educated herself through books, informational interviews, and hands-on experience. "I really had no idea what I was doing on the individual early-stage investing side," she admits. "I read a couple of books and tried to learn. It was during COVID, so I set up Zoom calls with whomever would talk to me about angel investing and just soaked all the information in."

As she gained experience, Mary's personal investment strategy began to evolve. She realized that while individual angel investments allowed her to support entrepreneurs directly, they also required a significant time commitment for due diligence and ongoing support. "I loved every bit of it," she says. "I called it playing with angel investing. That's what it was for me—learning something new."

As life returned to a new normal post-pandemic, Mary found her time increasingly constrained. This shift in circumstances prompted her to reassess her investment strategy. "I started realizing I no longer had the time to be doing individual angel investments," she reflects. "It made more sense to begin to consider venture fund investments, a strategy that involves investing in a portfolio rather than directly in individual companies." This pivot allowed Mary to harness the expertise of seasoned fund managers while maintaining her commitment to supporting a diverse array of startups. By investing in funds, she could extend her reach without sacrificing the quality of her investments or spreading herself too thin.

The transition to fund investing opened Mary's eyes to a broader perspective regarding startup. "I can see how these early-stage companies that I'm supporting on the angel side will later tie in to the fund strategy— they'll get the seed round from angel investors, but rounds two and three come from these funds that I'm aware of," she shares.

As her understanding of the angel investment landscape deepened, Mary recognized an opportunity. "I started realizing that a fund-of-funds approach could be even more expansive  because I could spread the dollars even farther," she explains.

This evolution to a fund-of-funds strategy allowed Mary to support not just individual companies or single funds but entire ecosystems of investors and entrepreneurs. It provided a way to address pervasive issues in funding. "If you look at the number of businesses that have gotten to Series A, Series B, and beyond that, the numbers start to drop off. So I'm most proud of my fund investments because I believe that's an important stepping stone."

When assessing potential investments, Mary looks beyond just the financials. "What is my intuition telling me about the lasting viability of this investment and its leadership team? she asks. She also considers whether the companies are adding real value to the world, with a particular focus on wellness in its broadest sense—including mental, emotional, spiritual, and financial health.

Mary stresses the importance of long-term commitment. "When you make an investment in a company, they're always going to come back to you and ask for more later," she notes. This realization has shaped her investment strategy, encouraging her to consider not just the initial investment but potential future rounds as well.

Today, Mary's professional journey has culminated in her role as Managing Director, Head of Responsible Investment Strategy at Antares Capital. She leverages her position to advocate for women in finance and promote responsible investing. She was vital in establishing the company's women's network and recently transitioned even further. "I moved into a corporate responsibility role, which is not only looking at the companies that we're lending to but also how we are really stepping into our own corporate responsibility as a business," she explains.

Mary is passionate about using her platform to support initiatives like *Show Her The Money* to amplify stories of women in investing. She is fueled by a desire to raise awareness about the disparities in venture capital funding for women-led businesses and to inspire change within the financial services industry. Looking to the future, Mary dreams of seeing more involvement from private credit and private equity firms in supporting early-stage, women-led businesses.

### Connect with Mary Rose

**100-CITY WORLDWIDE TOUR**

# FOUNDERS

# CHAPTER 29

# BUILDING A WORLDWIDE BEAUTY BRAND

**"SUCCESSFUL PEOPLE ARE NOT GIFTED, THEY JUST WORK HARD, THEN SUCCEED ON PURPOSE."**

- G.K. Neilson

**DIIPA BÜLLER-KHOSLA**

Founder/Cast

Bridging the worlds of ancient Ayurvedic wisdom and modern beauty innovation, Diipa Büller-Khosla has emerged as a trailblazing force in the global cosmetics industry. Her journey from aspiring lawyer to influential beauty mogul showcases the power of vision, adaptability, and cultural pride.

Her traditional Punjabi family upbringing instilled an entrepreneurial spirit in Diipa. "In our household, we were never told to go get a job," she recalls. "From a really young age, it was very instilled in me that you're going to go build something and create something." This mindset and her natural inclination towards business were early indicators of her future success.

As a child, Diipa filled her summers with new business ventures. She consistently demonstrated her entrepreneurial flair, from lemonade stands to more elaborate schemes. "Every summer holiday, I would have a new business plan," she laughs. "I would take my little sister as my employee and make my friends part of the whole thing."

Despite this early passion for business, Diipa initially pursued a more traditional path, studying law. However, a pivotal internship at an influencer agency in 2012 opened her eyes to a new world of possibilities. "I realized there's a lot of tailwinds around this new kind of industry," she explains. "The media landscape is changing, and I really need to be a part of it."

This realization led to a dramatic shift in her career trajectory. At 23, Diipa boldly decided to abandon her legal aspirations and dive headfirst into the world of influencing. "Everybody was shocked," she remembers. "They were like, 'Wait, aren't you such an academic? What are you doing?'"

But Diipa saw something others didn't. She recognized that democratizing media through social platforms was creating unprecedented opportunities. "I almost felt like somebody had whispered a secret to me early on," she says. "And it was now my duty to jump on this and see how far I could take it."

Her instincts proved prophetic. Diipa's online presence blossomed in the years that followed, catapulting her to the forefront of South Asian influencers. While her initial content centered on beauty and fashion, her raw, unfiltered sharing of her acne struggles truly captivated her audience. This vulnerable revelation struck a chord with followers worldwide, cementing her reputation for authenticity and deepening her connection with her growing community.

Recognizing the storytelling potential of her nuptials, Diipa strategically decided to share her wedding online. The event captivated an astonishing 200 million viewers, leaving India buzzing. "It was the first time, I think, when the country of India was like, 'Hold up, she's not really a socialite, but she's not really a Bollywood star. But why does she have so many people watching her?'" Diipa recalls. This calculated risk not only amplified her reach but, in her view, helped introduce and define the concept of the "influencer" in India, positioning her at the vanguard of a cultural shift.

As her influence grew, so did Diipa's vision for her future. During the pandemic, she took a step back to reassess her goals. "I've achieved everything I possibly had on my vision board as an influencer," she realized. "What's next?"

The answer came in the form of indē wild, a beauty brand that ingeniously fuses Diipa's rich cultural heritage with cutting-edge science. This venture wasn't merely a business opportunity but a culmination of generational wisdom and modern expertise. Diipa's mother, a dermatologist with deep knowledge of Ayurveda, had been creating skincare concoctions in their kitchen throughout Diipa's childhood. Their brand, indē wild, aimed to unlock the ancient secrets of Indian beauty rituals, backed by dermatological science, and present them to a global audience hungry for authentic, effective skincare solutions.

"It was going to be the first truly global Indian brand that would take India's secrets to the world," she explains. "It's never been done before."

Launching a brand during a pandemic was a risk, but Diipa's years of building trust with her audience paid off. The response was overwhelming when indē wild launched in November 2021 with just two products. "Within the first two minutes, 100 people made a purchase on our online store," Diipa recalls.

The success of indē wild is not just about celebrity endorsement. Diipa attributes it to the brand's authenticity and its alignment with the evolving identity of modern India. "It became so much bigger than me," she says. indē wild stood out by offering unprecedented transparency, being one of the first beauty brands in India to disclose percentages of active ingredients. "I think it was very refreshing for them to be like, 'Whoa, she has nothing to hide, and we see all the ingredients in both the products that I know will work for me,'" Diipa explains.

As the brand grew, Diipa faced new hurdles, especially regarding funding. "We knew nothing about investments, about VC. I had to Google what a VC even meant," she admits. Diipa and her husband initially invested their life savings to start the business. They turned to outside investment when they realized they needed more capital to match their ambitions.

A fortuitous connection with Rupa Ganatra, a woman Diipa had met at a speaking engagement at the House of Commons, opened doors to the world of angel investors. Rupa became a "fairy godmother," teaching Diipa the fundraising basics and introducing her to potential investors. Rupa's support led to their first round of funding from angel investors, which Diipa describes as a "friends and family" round, though it didn't actually involve their personal connections.

The success of their launch prompted Diipa to seek more substantial funding. Enter SoGal Ventures, a VC firm founded by Pocket Sun and Elizabeth Galbut, who were also featured alongside Diipa in the film, *Show Her The Money*. What was meant to be a brief 30-minute call turned into a two-and-a-half-hour conversation, during which Diipa felt an immediate connection with the SoGal team. "We realized we needed to level up, and we needed a VC like SoGal who believed in minority women businesses and really believed in our idea," Diipa explains. This alignment of values and vision made SoGal the perfect partner for indē wild's next phase of growth.

At the time of this interview, indē wild was closing another round of funding and planning for a potential Series A in 18 months to two years.

For aspiring founders, especially women, Diipa's advice is clear: "The most important thing is to trust yourself and believe in yourself. I think women, for some reason, so much more than men, have Imposter Syndrome. Just take that first step, and you'll keep figuring it out."

Looking to the future, Diipa remains focused on growing indē wild, with profitability as the next primary goal. While an exit strategy isn't off the table, for now she's content to see where this journey takes her. "It's just two and a half years in," she says. "Let's see where it goes."

Diipa Büller-Khosla's story is about cultural pride, entrepreneurial spirit, and the power of seizing opportunities. Her journey inspires hopeful founders everywhere, proving that with vision, determination, and a willingness to take risks, it's possible to create something truly transformative.

### Connect with Diipa Büller-Khosla

**COMPANIES FOUNDED BY WOMEN OUTPERFORMED COMPANIES FOUNDED BY MEN BY 63% IN CREATING VALUE FOR INVESTORS.**

Source: First Round Capital

# CHAPTER 30

# DEMOCRATIZING AN INDUSTRY

"WE'RE HERE TO
PUT A DENT IN
THE UNIVERSE.
OTHERWISE
WHY ELSE EVEN
BE HERE."
- Steve Jobs


H SCHUSTER

Founder/Cast

H Schuster's path to becoming a venture-backed tech founder began not in Silicon Valley, but in the vibrant theater scene of New York City. As a college student at NYU, while her peers were focused on their studies, H was already immersing herself in the world of professional theater.

"I was very fortunate because I worked to help put myself through college. I had an academic scholarship at NYU, then worked to pay my way," H reflects. This early exposure to the inner workings of prestigious institutions like the Public Theater, New Dramatists, and The New York Theatre Workshop laid the foundation for a career that would span academia, entertainment, and eventually, tech entrepreneurship.

H's journey from theater professional to pioneering force in venture capital is a testament to the power of identifying systemic problems and leveraging diverse experiences to create innovative solutions. Her time in New York's theater world, working on groundbreaking premiere productions like *Angels in America and Rent*, instilled in her a deep appreciation for nurturing new talent and providing platforms for fresh voices—themes that would resurface years later in her tech venture.

After receiving her PhD from NYU, where she taught theater and cinema studies, H made a bold move to the West Coast. There, she pursued a law degree at Stanford, further diversifying her skill set. Armed with this unique combination of theater expertise, academic credentials, and legal knowledge, H pivoted to the world of film and television.

It was during her years working in Hollywood as a C-suite executive and executive producer that H identified a critical issue in the industry: the antiquated and inefficient process of sourcing and staffing freelance creative talent. "It was a very painful, laborious analog process. And as a function of that, the same people got hired over and over again. And, you know, it often was not a particularly diverse crew," H explains. This observation, viewed through the lens of her own diverse experiences, became the catalyst for HUSSLUP, a platform designed to revolutionize how creative talent is discovered and hired in the entertainment industry.

"TechCrunch has called us LinkedIn for the entertainment biz. We're trying to build efficiencies so that studios and production companies can staff more diverse, better talent, more efficiently, and save money in the process; and our freelancers can connect with jobs and opportunities more efficiently, have less downtime, and upskill to get to the next level of their career more quickly," H explains. "Our mission is to democratize access to the industry."

Launching HUSSLUP presented H with her biggest challenge yet. "I started this as a solo founder, without a technical and engineering co-founder," she candidly admits. This meant navigating the complex world of product development, engineering, and venture capital fundraising without the technical background often found in tech startups.

H's first foray into venture capital came through a methodical approach to fundraising. The company's first big break came when it was accepted into the NBCU LIFT Labs Accelerator powered by Techstars. This program provided an initial investment and launched HUSSLUP's pre-seed round. Following this, H raised capital from angel investors and VCs, demonstrating her growing savvy in the startup world. H also received funding from investor Dawn Lafreeda during the *Show Her The Money* Pitch Fest.

"We made a commitment going into the seed round that we were only going to raise from diverse VCs, which made it a lot harder, but we felt that they would share our mission and share our vision," H reflects. This decision, while challenging, helped them find partners that aligned with HUSSLUP's values, which proved to be a strategic advantage.

The fundraising process taught H valuable lessons about the venture capital world. "It's a process that you have to run like a business," she advises. "You have to be very methodical about creating your pipeline, timing things out, and following up to create momentum to get checks in the door."

H also noticed gender disparities in how founders are perceived by investors. She was deeply influenced by an insight from another female founder: "When women are in their first meeting, or any meeting, really, the VC often frames the questions as, 'Why will you fail?' 'Why can't you do this?' And with male founders, it tends to be blue sky, like, tell us all the great things that you're doing." This observation led H to adapt her pitching strategy, focusing on turning negative questions into positive answers and emphasizing the potential for growth and success.

As HUSSLUP looks to the future, H acknowledges the need to balance its mission with financial viability. "We're at a point now in our life cycle where we do need to see studios or production companies paying," she states, highlighting the shift towards monetization as a critical juncture for securing additional funding.

For founders seeking investment, H offers this advice: "Engage at a time when you don't need the capital. Build relationships so that when you do need the capital, the VCs are teed up." She notes that approaching investors from a place of strength positions you to be more memorable and build more lasting relationships.

H's vision for HUSSLUP's legacy is clear and inspiring. "I hope that HUSSLUP can be seen as a platform that wants to make the industry better for everyone," she says. By improving efficiency and expanding access, H aims to increase diversity in the hiring pipeline and help talented individuals break into an industry often perceived as gated, just like the studio lots.

H Schuster's journey from theater enthusiast to tech founder exemplifies the power of identifying systemic problems and leveraging diverse experiences to create innovative solutions. Through HUSSLUP, she is not just building a company; she's working to reshape an entire industry, making it more accessible, efficient, and equitable for all, while paving the way for more diverse voices in both entertainment and tech entrepreneurship.

## Connect with H Schuster

# CHAPTER 31

# REVOLUTIONARY PRODUCTS THAT IMPACT CHANGE

# "MY MISSION IN LIFE IS NOT MERELY TO SURVIVE, BUT TO THRIVE."

- Maya Angelou

## JASMINE JONES

Founder/Cast

When Jasmine Jones was just nine years old, she discovered her grandmother's prosthetic breasts in a drawer. She learned that her grandmother, a vibrant and free-spirited woman, only wore her prosthetics for special occasions because they didn't match her skin tone and didn't fit well, leaving her self-conscious.

This memory stayed with Jasmine, influencing her perspective as she grew older. Years later, as a college student in North Carolina, she encountered a petition urging Victoria's Secret to acknowledge breast cancer survivors by offering mastectomy bras. The lingerie giant's refusal sparked something in Jasmine. "Someone should do something about it," she thought, not yet realizing she would become that someone. These experiences—her childhood observations and the Victoria's Secret petition—would ultimately converge to inspire Jasmine's revolutionary business idea.

After college, Jasmine's career took her to Nordstrom, where she quickly rose from intern to manager at just 22 years old. This experience in retail would prove invaluable in her future endeavors. However, a chance encounter at a breast cancer awareness 5K event would set her on the path to creating Cherry Blossom Intimates, which would later evolve into Myya.

At the 5K, Jasmine met Dr. Regina Hampton, a breast surgeon struggling to find post-mastectomy products for her patients. This meeting was serendipitous—Jasmine had almost missed the event because her Uber driver got lost. "Fix your attitude," she told herself as she arrived late. "You never know who you're going to meet today." Those words proved prophetic as she and Dr. Hampton soon partnered to open a boutique specializing in post-mastectomy care. "The money I was going to actually spend to go to Harvard and get an MBA—I ended up putting into the business, and the rest is history."

Cherry Blossom Intimates, their brick-and-mortar boutique, opened its doors during Breast Cancer Awareness Month in 2018. The boutique included a medical component, which quickly gained traction. "We noticed very quickly that that side of the business was growing very fast, expanding very fast," Jasmine recalls. "We had a lot of patients reaching out to us from all over the country. They wanted to be able to shop with dignity for post-mastectomy bras and breast forms."

However, Jasmine and her team quickly encountered stumbling blocks. The sizes offered by existing brands were limited, and the prosthetics came in just one skin tone—a problem for their diverse clientele in Prince George's County, Maryland. Additionally, the business model itself proved challenging; while they accepted insurance, the reimbursement rates for post-mastectomy products left razor-thin margins, making it difficult to sustain the business on product sales alone. These limitations, amplified by the effects of the COVID-19 pandemic forced her to pivot her business model.

With patients unable to visit the store, she innovated a new approach to serving them. "I was doing video visits on Zoom with our patients who were locked into their homes during the pandemic," Jasmine explains. "We'd measure them virtually, talk about their lifestyle, and then I would drive to their home and drop off a box of bras and breast forms."

This personalized service didn't end with delivery. Jasmine would follow up with another video visit, guiding patients on putting on their bras and wearing the prosthetics properly. This hands-on, yet virtual approach allowed Cherry Blossom Intimates to continue serving their clients during unprecedented times.

After Jasmine performed about 90 of these virtual fittings, she had an epiphany: "I recognized that this could be a business of its own," she says. With that, Cherry Blossom Intimates became Myya—a groundbreaking solution in the post-mastectomy care industry. Jasmine describes it as "a first-of-its-kind, fully encompassing direct-to-consumer post-mastectomy care brand that offers in-person and video visit experiences for breast cancer survivors."

Drawing a parallel to innovative companies in other sectors, Jasmine explains, "We're much like the Warby Parker of boobs." Myya's unique offering includes wholly customizable and fully insurance-billable breast prostheses and a state-of-the-art fit experience. This experience has expanded to include telehealth consultations and pop-up events across the United States, making their services more accessible than ever.

Jasmine's journey into venture capital was as unexpected as her entry into the post-mastectomy care industry. A chance meeting with female venture capitalist, Pocket Sun, at Forbes 30 Under 30 in Israel opened her eyes to the possibility of funding. This connection proved pivotal when Pocket invited Jasmine to pitch Myya at an upcoming event. Despite having no prior knowledge of pitch decks or startup jargon, Jasmine accepted the invitation and dove headfirst into the world of fundraising.

As a former holder of the Miss District of Columbia title, Jasmine drew upon her experience and prepared for her first pitch competition as she would for a pageant. Her unique approach won her $100,000 from SoGal Ventures and an invitation to the TechStars accelerator program. This success catapulted Myya into a new phase of growth, with Jasmine raising over $2 million in venture capital and winning an additional $300,000 in pitch competitions.

The capital infusion allowed Myya to innovate rapidly, staying ahead of competitors in areas like diversity, size-inclusivity, and modernizing the ordering process. "We had a running start," Jasmine explains. "Our brand was really beautiful, accessible, and friendly, and it just allowed us to grow really quickly."

However, Jasmine found it challenging to manage investor expectations and navigate the complexities of scaling a healthcare-adjacent business. "Everything costs more than you expect," she advises new founders. "Build in at least 30% more equity than you expect to need."

Through it all, Jasmine has remained committed to serving breast cancer survivors with dignity and innovation. Her journey, including the ups and downs of entrepreneurship and personal life, being captured in *Show Her The Money* has helped spread Myya's message even further.

Looking to the future, Jasmine aims to serve a million breast cancer survivors. She sees partnerships with larger organizations as key to achieving this goal. Despite discussions about exit strategies, Jasmine remains passionate about the work. "I enjoy what we do. I enjoy this space and I want to continue to do it," she says.

For Jasmine, building Myya is about more than just business success. It's about creating a legacy and setting an example for her young daughter. "I want her to continue to see women as entrepreneurs, women leaders," Jasmine explains.

Her most treasured biblical passage, Philippians 4:13—"I can do all things through Christ who gives me strength"—has been a constant source of motivation.

Jasmine's story is a powerful reminder of how personal experiences can fuel innovation and drive positive change. From observing her grandmother's struggle as a child to building a tech-enabled company revolutionizing post-mastectomy care, Jasmine's journey embodies the transformative power of purpose-driven entrepreneurship.

## Connect with Jasmine Jones

# CHAPTER 32

## A PIONEERING FORCE

# "YOU GAIN STRENGTH, COURAGE AND CONFIDENCE BY EVERY EXPERIENCE IN WHICH YOU REALLY STOP TO LOOK FEAR IN THE FACE."

- Eleanor Roosevelt

## MARIAN LEITNER-WALDMAN

Founder/Cast

In the competitive world of wine and venture capital, Marian Leitner-Waldman stands out as a pioneering force. As the founder and CEO of Archer Roose Wines, she's changing how we consume wine and challenging the status quo in startup funding for women entrepreneurs.

Marian's journey to becoming a funded wine entrepreneur is as unconventional as her approach to the industry. Growing up in New York City, she was raised in a household that valued activism and entrepreneurship. This upbringing laid the foundation for Marian's future endeavors, shaping her into someone who would seek to make a difference through innovative business practices.

After studying International Studies at Johns Hopkins University, Marian's career path weaved through finance, literary publishing, and global health. She worked on projects ranging from microinsurance for migrant workers to vaccine distribution in developing countries. These experiences, while seemingly unrelated to wine, provided her with a global perspective and a deep understanding of how businesses can address social issues.

While on a ski trip with her husband, Marian craved wine while her husband was having a can of beer, but she didn't want to open a whole bottle for just one glass and have the rest go to waste. This common dilemma led Marian to question the standard 750ml bottle format. "Literally, the bottle serves five glasses of wine. It doesn't make any sense," she decided.

Her curiosity piqued, she began investigating the wine industry and discovered some interesting facts. "First of all, 97% of consumers buy wine and consume it within 72 hours after purchase," Marian learned. Furthermore, "60% of municipalities in the United States don't recycle glass at all," highlighting a significant environmental issue with traditional wine bottles.

Moreover, the wine aisle and wine menus are confusing for consumers. The industry has truly commodified products, stressing winemaking techniques versus consumer values and insights to create a relationship with drinkers. She saw an opportunity to build a modern wine brand built on transparency, and sustainability.

Marian dreamed of creating a high-qualtiy wine brand in convenient and perfectly-portioned packaging. Her husband's experience rehabilitating a dilapidated winery in the Republic of Georgia uncovered the unused capacity in wine production, which led her to develop a capital-light business plan.

The result was Archer Roose Wines, which packages wine in cans and kegs, allowing consumers to enjoy premium wine without the waste or commitment of a full bottle. Marian's innovative approach to packaging and distribution formed the foundation for Archer Roose Wine's unique position in the market.

When Marian first sought funding for Archer Roose Wines, she encountered the harsh realities of the venture capital world. "I started reaching out to friends and family. But you know, that really wasn't a big avenue that was open," she recalls.

The journey to secure funding was fraught with obstacles and biases. Marian recounts her experiences pitching to angel groups: "I got asked, 'Oh, you're newly married. When are you going to get pregnant?'" Such questions, irrelevant to her business acumen or Archer Roose Wine's potential, underscore the additional and unnecessary scrutiny women entrepreneurs often face.

Marian's approach to building Archer Roose Wines while seeking funding was pragmatic and cautious. She built the company for two years while maintaining her day job at the World Bank—a strategy reflecting some of her essential advice for aspiring entrepreneurs: "Don't quit your day job just yet. Nothing is more important than paying your rent." She didn't leave the World Bank until she had 24,000 liters of wine and had raised initial funding.

The first few years of Archer Roose Wines were, in Marian's words, "just an effing slog." "'Become a founder,' they said, 'It'll be glamorous,' they said... as I'm lugging boxes, knocking on doors, and driving around random parts of the state to build distribution," she wryly quips. She was running supply chain, selling wine, and doing everything herself. But as she gained traction in bars, restaurants, and hospitality spaces, she began building a reputation to help her secure more substantial funding.

A significant turning point came when Marian finally raised her first seed round for Archer Roose Wines. The following year brought even more success: "In 2019, Archer Roose Wines won a blind taste test against 30 other brands, and it was selected to be carried by JetBlue airlines. With this deal in hand, I raised a million and a half dollars, led by SoGal Ventures. They were my first institutional funding."

SoGal's investment was a game-changer for Marian. She speaks highly of the SoGal founders: "Wherever Pocket Sun and Elizabeth Galbut lead, I will follow because they care about their founders. They pay for executive coaching for many of their portfolio companies, and considering what a grind this is, that's how you build and develop stamina in a business." This kind of comprehensive backing makes a crucial difference for startups.

However, just as Archer Roose Wines seemed poised for takeoff, the COVID-19 pandemic hit. This crisis threatened to derail the business Marian had worked so hard to build and made the value of having supportive investors crystal clear. "By that point, I had some really thoughtful people on my capitalization table who had seen what I had done over the last couple of years and knew that I wasn't going to give up," Marian reflects.

Her resilience paid off. Marian deftly pivoted the company's focus to grocery and off-premise sales and reached out to Elizabeth Banks, whom she had long envisioned as an ideal partner. Impressed by Marian's plans for Archer Roose Wines, Banks joined as chief creative officer. These strategic moves, bolstered by her investors' unwavering faith, set the stage for Archer Roose Wine's remarkable growth trajectory.

Today, Archer Roose is a success story in both the wine and venture capital worlds. Over the last three years, Marian has raised over $20 million, including an investment from Constellation Brands, the US's largest publicly traded wine and spirits company.

Marian emphasizes the importance of drive and perseverance as an entrepreneur, noting that it took her seven years to raise her first $5 million. "There's this perception that success is overnight in startups. Not true. I can't tell you how many founders I have connected with that speak about their 'overnight success'... ten years in the making," she reflects.

Marian's experiences have made her a vocal advocate for increasing access to capital for women and underrepresented founders. She points out the dark reality, "It's abhorrent, the miniscule amount of venture funding that goes to women." She sees this not just as an issue of fairness but as a critical factor in shaping the future. "The only way that we're ever going to achieve equality is by increasing access to capital and the ability to accumulate wealth."

Marian's ambitions for the future are bold. "I want to build a billion-dollar brand," she declares. But her vision goes beyond mere financial success. She wants Archer Roose Wines to be a force of change in both the wine industry and the venture capital world. And she is well on her way.

Connect with Marian Leitner-Waldman

# CHAPTER 33

# REVOLUTIONIZING
# RETAIL

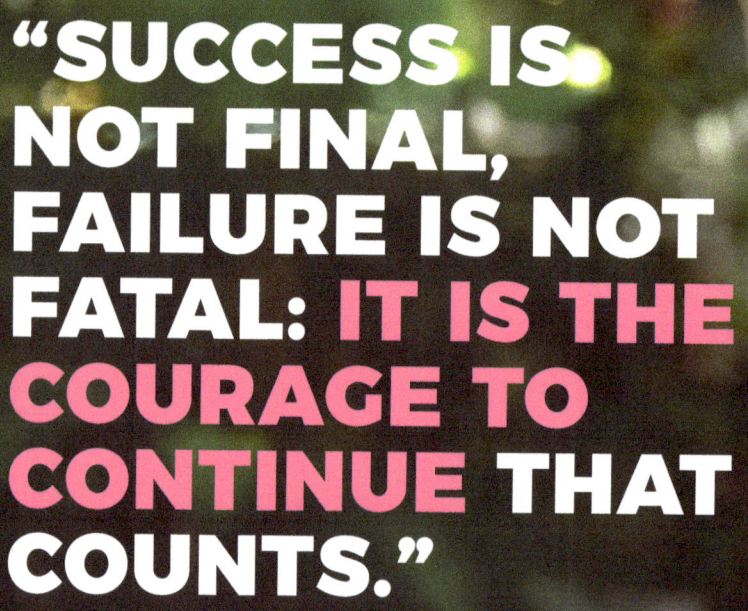

**"SUCCESS IS NOT FINAL, FAILURE IS NOT FATAL: IT IS THE COURAGE TO CONTINUE THAT COUNTS."**

- Winston Churchill

**VICKY PASCHE**

Founder/Cast

In the heart of San Diego, Vicky Pasche stands at the intersection of fashion and social change, weaving a narrative that confronts cultural expectations one stitch at a time. As the co-founder and CEO of Dapper Boi, an all-gender, size-inclusive clothing brand, Vicky's journey from casino manager to trailblazing entrepreneur exemplifies the transformative power of authenticity and persistence.

Growing up in upstate New York, young Vicky was a self-proclaimed tomboy and jock. Her childhood was filled with sports and creative ventures, including making homemade commercials with friends. This early experience with creativity and self-expression foreshadowed her future as an entrepreneur who would challenge traditional conventions in the fashion industry.

The seeds of Dapper Boi were sown in the most unlikely of places—the men's department of clothing stores. As a woman who preferred masculine styles, Vicky found herself constantly struggling to find clothes that fit both her body and her identity. "You walk into a department store, and you literally have two options, the men's section and the women's section, which are really embedded with the societal rules based on your gender. I hated shopping because it was never me," she recalls.

The turning point came when Vicky's wife, Charisse, attempted to help. "She's a fashionista," Vicky explains, "she would buy me all these clothes off the rack, thinking this is going to solve the problem, that I was just picking the wrong things. But that wasn't the case at all. The clothes just never fit me." This realization led to a profound epiphany: they weren't alone in this struggle.

In 2015, Vicky and Charisse took a leap of faith, launching Dapper Boi on Kickstarter with a single pair of jeans. Their goal was to raise $18,000; they ended up with over $26,000. This success was more than just financial—it validated a need in the market that had long gone unaddressed.

The journey, however, was far from smooth. The couple faced numerous challenges as they bootstrapped their way forward, using a pre-order model to fund production and growth. Their innovative approach paid off, with Dapper Boi hitting $1 million in sales by 2020.

As the business grew, so did the pressure to maintain momentum and secure funding. Vicky found herself navigating the complex world of investors and capital—a world she was initially intimidated by. "I didn't grow up with money," she admits. "And so talking to investors was a very intimidating thing." This intimidation led to some missteps, including falling into the trap of predatory merchant cash advances.

As if by fate, Vicky's path intersected once again with Catherine Gray, whom she had first met years earlier at a pop-up event. After their initial encounter, they had connected online, with Vicky following Catherine's career from afar. As Dapper Boi faced growing pains, Vicky noticed Catherine offered a course called, "Six Ways to Fund Your Business." Intrigued, Vicky enrolled in the course, finding it both informative and inspiring.

"I took the course. I loved it. I messaged her," Vicky recalls, which opened the door to a pivotal conversation in which Vicky mentioned Dapper Boi's search for investors. Catherine, recognizing the potential in Vicky's story and brand, made a crucial introduction, connecting Vicky with Ky Dickens, a director working with Catherine on a documentary about women investing in women entrepreneurs.

What Vicky initially thought might be an investor pitch opportunity turned out to be something far more significant when Catherine and Ky invited Vicky and Charisse to be featured in *Show Her The Money*, an experience that would prove transformative for both the couple and their business.

"The universe brings people into your lives that should be in your life," Vicky muses, emphasizing how seemingly small connections can lead to significant opportunities. Participating in the documentary not only provided invaluable exposure but also opened doors to a new network of investors and mentors.

The filming process captured some of Dapper Boi's most challenging times, including financial struggles and difficult decisions. This vulnerability, shared on camera, resonated deeply with viewers and potential investors alike. "It was very hard for us to share," Vicky admits, "but by being able to share our story and knowing the impact that we have on others who are going through the same thing, it was worth it to us."

Through *Show Her The Money*, Vicky gained a new perspective on dealing with investors. "They're just not as scary as I thought they were," she reflects. "They are just people like me." This newfound outlook would prove crucial as Vicky and Charisse faced their next big obstacle.

In 2021, Vicky and Charisse applied to appear on *Shark Tank*. Months later, they received a life-changing call. Vicky recalls the morning of their appearance: "We had $100 to our name: Dapper Boi, personal, everything." Just hours before facing the Sharks, they received a lifeline—a $250,000 check from investor Kelly Ann Winget, whom they'd met through Catherine.

Despite their preparation, the Sharks didn't grasp Dapper Boi's full potential, so none invested; however, it was great publicity, and the exposure boosted their sales, so Vicky sees it as a net positive experience. "I'm glad we didn't get one of the sharks because I don't think they got it. For us, it's not about creating this third category that is way too exclusive. We're not trying to be in the pride section during the month of June.

The impact of *Show Her The Money* has extended far beyond the film itself. Vicky found that the documentary continued to yield unexpected benefits long after its completion. Moreover, some of the investors featured in the documentary were so impressed by Dapper Boi's story and business model that they became actual backers of the company. This tangible support underscored the power of authentic storytelling in attracting not just customers but also investors who believe in the brand's mission.

As Dapper Boi continues to grow, Vicky and Charisse remain committed to their vision. "It's really about clothing being about style preference and body type, not gender," she explains. This perspective has caught the attention of major retailers, with Nordstrom recently agreeing to carry Dapper Boi products online. Additionally, with plans for expansion into other countries like Canada, the UK, Australia, and others, their goal is to become a 100 million dollar business.

Vicky's path offers valuable lessons for aspiring entrepreneurs. She stresses the importance of connecting early with potential investors and mentors, understanding one's exit strategy, and recognizing different types of capital. Most importantly, she encourages founders to get out of their own way. "When you're asking for money, you're not asking for yourself, you're asking for your people, your customers, your why," she advises.

Vicky's story is more than just a business success—it's a powerful illustration of authenticity and tenacity in the face of adversity. With each garment, partnership, and milestone, she and Charisse are not just building a brand—they are fostering a movement that challenges us to rethink the very fabric of fashion and identity. "We believe with every part of our being that we are the next Levi's of All-Gender fashion."

### Connect with Vicky Pasche

# SUMMARY

# CATHERINE GRAY
## PRODUCER

## JOINING THE MOVIE-MENT!!

As we reach the end of this journey through the stories of these remarkable women founders and funders, I hope you have been as inspired by these stories as I have.

The passion, creativity, and brilliance of these women have not only changed their own lives but are reshaping the entire landscape of venture capital and entrepreneurship.

## THE ROAD AHEAD

Change is possible, as these stories have told us.

At the rate we were going, women would only receive 20% of venture capital funding by 2050. That's simply not good enough. But by accelerating our Movie-ment, raising awareness, and educating women about this asset class to inspire them to invest in venture capital, we can get there much faster!

I see a world brimming with brilliant innovations and game-changing ideas born from tapping into the full potential of all entrepreneurs, regardless of their gender, race, or background.

This vision fuels our mission to transform the world of venture capital.

As we close this book, I want you to remember that you are now part of this Movie-ment.

Now, you can help us carry this torch forward with determination and unstoppable grit.

With women coming into trillions of dollars in the coming decade—we simply need to educate them on the value of impact investing in venture capital to solve this issue. With the biggest transfer of wealth in history coming to women—we have the wind at our backs. Plus, many qualified women investors in the C-suites, together with many new male allies, gives us an opportunity to vote with our money to achieve gender equity. This will, in turn, build more generational wealth and will positively impact the world at large. We will all gain from innovations created by all types of people—including women, BIPOC and LGBTQ founders with game-changing ideas that will benefit all of humanity.

## RESOURCES TO GET STARTED:

Now that you've read these inspiring stories, you might be wondering, "How do I get involved? How can I become part of this Movie-ment?" The good news is there are many ways to contribute, regardless of your background or circumstances. You can visit our resources page www.ShowHerTheMoneyMovie.com and join our community newsletter for updates.

# AS YOU KNOW, THIS IS A MOVIE AND A MOVEMENT. HERE ARE 10 WAYS TO SUPPORT OUR MOVIE-MENT!

1. **Educate Yourself:** Keep learning about venture capital and the challenges women and underrepresented groups face in this field. The more you know, the more effectively you can advocate for change. Our website resources page has recommended books, podcasts, workshops and more to educate you and your circle of friends.

2. **Spread the Word:** Share the stories from this book with your network. Use social media, book clubs, or community gatherings to discuss the issues raised and brainstorm solutions. Tag us @showherthemoney on Instagram, LinkedIn and Facebook.

3. **Support Women-Led Businesses:** Make conscious choices to support businesses founded or led by women, especially in your local community.

4. **Invest in Women Founders:** If you have the means, consider becoming an angel investor or joining a venture capital fund focusing on women-led startups. Remember, you don't need millions to start—even small investments can make a big difference. This can be done by investing as little as $25 in a crowdfunding campaign for a women-led startup through platforms like WeFunder, Republic or others.

5. **Become a Mentor:** If you have experience in business or entrepreneurship, consider mentoring a woman who is just starting her journey.

6. **Be An Advocate:** Use your voice to advocate for policies that support women in business and venture capital within your workplace, your community, or even at a national level.

7. **Join or Create Networks:** Look for organizations in your area that support women in business and venture capital. If there aren't any, consider starting one!

8. **Create or Attend Events:** Attend venture capital and entrepreneurship events, especially those focused on diversity and inclusion.

9. **Attend Screenings:** Look out for screenings of *Show Her The Money* in your area or book a live or virtual screening on our site www.ShowHerTheMoneyMovie.com

10. **Be a Connector:** Introduce a female founder and a potential investor or mentor—this costs nothing but can be invaluable!

## A BRIGHT FUTURE AHEAD

You have seen what these incredible women have achieved, often against significant odds. You have witnessed the power of determination, innovation, and support. Now, it's your turn to carry this torch forward.

None of us know how long we have on this planet—but while we are here, we can live with purpose and contribute to this change. The future of innovation, business, and our world depends on everyone working together to ensure everyone has a seat at the table.

# REFERENCES & RESOURCES

# EXPLORE FURTHER: YOUR GATEWAY TO ACTION

Here is a comprehensive list of resources to help guide your next steps to the world of venture capital and entrepreneurship.

Visit www.ShowHerTheMoneyMovie.com or Scan this QR code for access to the following:

- Funds and projects led by the visionaries featured in this book
- Educational programs and workshops on investing and entrepreneurship
- Recommended books, podcasts, and media for continued learning
- Networking events and investment opportunities
- Tools and platforms for aspiring entrepreneurs

# BOOK GLOSSARY

**Accredited Investor:** An individual or entity that meets specific financial criteria established by regulatory authorities, such as the U.S. Securities and Exchange Commission (SEC), allowing them to invest in private market opportunities not available to the general public. These opportunities often include private equity, venture capital, hedge funds, and other alternative investments that carry higher risks.

To qualify as an accredited investor in the United States, an individual must meet at least one of the following criteria:

- Income: Have an annual income exceeding $200,000 (or $300,000 jointly with a spouse or partner) for the past two years, with a reasonable expectation of maintaining that income.
- Net Worth: Possess a net worth of over $1 million, either alone or together with a spouse or spousal equivalent, excluding the value of the person's primary residence.
- Professional Certifications: Hold in good standing a Series 7, 65, or 82 license.

Entities such as banks, investment firms, and certain organizations may also qualify if they meet established financial thresholds. Accredited investors are presumed to have the financial knowledge and resources to bear the risks associated with unregistered securities.

*Source: U.S. Securities and Exchange Commission (Accredited Investors)*

**Angel Investing:** Angel Investing involves individual investors, known as "angel investors," who provide capital to startups or small businesses, usually in exchange for equity or convertible debt. Angel investors typically invest their personal funds and are often among the first external investors in a company, taking on significant risk in exchange for the potential of high returns. Unlike venture capitalists, angel investors often invest smaller amounts and may also provide mentorship and networking opportunities.

*Source: Investopedia (Angel Investor Definition)*

**Donor-Advised Fund (DAF):** A charitable giving vehicle administered by a public charity. It allows donors to make charitable contributions, receive an immediate tax deduction, and then recommend grants to qualified charities over time. Donors can contribute various assets, such as cash, securities, or other property, and the funds can be invested for potential growth. While donors retain advisory privileges regarding grant distributions, the sponsoring organization has legal control over the funds.

*Source: Internal Revenue Service (Donor-Advised Funds)*

**Exit:** The process by which the owners of a business realize the value of their investment by selling the company or its assets. This can involve selling the entire company, a controlling interest, or specific assets to another business, private equity firm, or individual investors. Common types of exits include acquisitions, mergers, or initial public offerings (IPOs). An exit is often a key goal for startups and small businesses seeking to provide a return on investment for founders and investors.

*Source: Investopedia (Exit Definition)*

**Fintech:** Financial technology (fintech) refers to new technology that seeks to improve and automate the delivery and use of financial services. At its core, fintech is utilized to help companies, business owners, and consumers better manage their financial operations, processes, and lives. It is composed of specialized software and algorithms used on computers and smartphones.

*Source: Investopedia (Fintech Definition)*

**Founder:** Or entrepreneur is an individual who establishes a company, typically responsible for forming its vision, mission, and initial structure. Founders often drive early growth and set the strategic direction.

*Source: Investopedia (Entrepreneur Definition)*

**Funder:** An investor is an individual or entity that provides financial support to a business or organization, typically through investment or grants, to fuel its operations or expansion.

*Source: Investopedia (Sources of Funding Available for Companies)*

**General Partner (GP):** The manager of a partnership, often in venture capital or private equity, who has unlimited liability and actively manages the investment activities. GPs are responsible for investment decisions and overseeing the fund's operations.

*Source: Investopedia (General Partner Definition)*

**Limited Partner (LP):** An investor in a partnership, usually a venture capital or private equity fund, who contributes capital but has limited liability. LPs have no management authority and are not responsible for day-to-day operations, minimizing their risk exposure.

*Source: Carta (Limited Partner Definition)*

**Pre-seed Funding:** A pre-seed round is the earliest stage of startup funding, often used to turn an idea into a working prototype or business plan. At this stage, companies typically have little to no revenue, and funding comes from the founders, friends, family, or angel investors who believe in the concept. The capital is usually used for product development, market research, and initial business operations.

*Source: DigitalOcean (What Is Pre-Seed Funding?)*

**Private Equity (PE):** Refers to investments made directly into private companies (or in publicly traded companies to take them private) with the goal of acquiring ownership and increasing the company's value over time. Private equity firms pool funds from institutional investors and high-net-worth individuals to purchase and manage companies, often through leveraged buyouts (LBOs). These investments are typically focused on more mature businesses and aim to improve operational efficiency and profitability before selling the company for a profit.

*Source: Investopedia (Private Equity Definition)*

**Seed Round:** A seed round is the first official funding stage, where a startup raises money to develop its product, conduct market research, and build its team. Investors at this stage often include angel investors, venture capital firms, or even friends and family.

*Source: Investopedia (Seed Funding Definition)*

**Series A:** A Series A round helps a startup scale its business after proving product-market fit. The funding is used to expand operations, hire key employees, and optimize the business model for long-term growth. Investors are usually venture capital firms looking for high-growth potential.

*Source: Forbes (What Is Series A Funding?)*

**Series B:** A Series B round funds the next stage of growth, focusing on scaling operations, entering new markets, and increasing revenue. Startups at this stage have a proven business model and need capital to expand their customer base and infrastructure.

*Source: Crunchbase (Series B Funding Explained)*

**Series C:** A Series C round is for mature startups looking to expand globally, develop new products, or even acquire other companies. These companies are often on the path to an IPO or major acquisition, attracting larger investors like hedge funds and private equity firms.

*Source: TechCrunch (Series C Funding Overview)*

**Special Purpose Vehicle (SPV):** A legal entity created for a specific business purpose, usually to isolate financial risk. SPVs are commonly used in investments, mergers, and acquisitions to structure transactions while limiting liability.

*Source: Investopedia (Special Purpose Vehicle (SPV) Definition)*

**Venture Capital (VC):** Refers to funding provided by investors to startups and early-stage companies with high growth potential but also significant risk. Venture capital is typically exchanged for equity or an ownership stake in the company. In addition to funding, VC investors often provide strategic guidance, mentorship, and industry connections to help businesses scale, particularly in innovative sectors like technology, healthcare, or clean energy.

*Source: Wikipedia (Venture Capital Definition)*

# FUNDS FOR INVESTORS AND FOUNDERS

### Alternative Wealth Partners
www.alternativewealthpartners.com

Alternative Wealth Partners (AWP), led by Kelly Ann Winget, specializes in diversified private equity investments, targeting sectors typically overlooked by traditional banks. AWP champions an inclusive and educational approach, democratizing access to alternative investments. The firm's strategy emphasizes diversification and social responsibility, aiming to achieve robust economic growth and meaningful community impact.

Email: info@alternativewealthpartners.com

### Emmeline Ventures
www.emmelineventures.vc

Emmeline Ventures is a group of investors steadfastly committed to investing in and serving as catalysts for new, emerging founders & businesses. They invest in female founders building game-changing businesses which empower women, in particular, to manage their health, build their wealth, and live in a cleaner, safer world.

Email: team@emmelineventures.vc

### Enygma Ventures
www.enygmaventures.com

At Enygma, they strongly believe that the investment finance industry needs to be globally reimagined. Their aim is to empower women to help create a more equitable playing field, drive progressive change, and still achieve exceptional outcomes. Their goal is not only to demonstrate that there is a better way, but also to inspire others to do the same.

Email: info@enygmaventures.com

### Gaingels
www.gaingels.com

Gaingels co-invests with select venture capital leads in companies resolved on building diverse and inclusive teams. They seek to drive top returns while influencing the ecosystem and representing the LGBTQ community, its allies, and a diverse group of investors within the capital stack of its portfolio companies.

Email: jennifer@gaingels.com

### Portola Valley Partners
www.portolavalleypartners.com

Portola Valley Partners' unique investment methodology can substantially increase a company's success rate. Staffed with investors, entrepreneurs, inventors, and former big-tech executives, these hands-on operators help ensure success.

Email: venture@portolavalleypartners.com

### She Angel Investors
www.sheangelinvestors.com

She Angel Investors works to connect women entrepreneurs and investors through their multi-media platform.

Email: contact@sheangelinvestors.com

### SoGal Ventures
www.sogalventures.com

SoGal Ventures represents how far their generation has come and how deep their impact on the world can be. They are investing in next-gen billion-dollar businesses that unapologetically benefit people, society, and the planet.

Email: hello@sogalventures.com

### Stella
www.stella.co

Stella supports the female entrepreneurial journey at every stage by providing rigorous action-based business training programs, high-touch mentorship, curated consulting services, and access to capital.
Join the free community at community.stella.com

Email: info@stella.co

## WOMEN'S EMPOWERMENT WORKSHOPS AND COMMUNITIES

### The BRA Network
www.bra-network.com

Carrie Murray

The Business Relationship Alliance (BRA) Network's mission is to foster a community to uplift female and non-binary entrepreneurs and provide support, resources, and opportunities for connection in an inclusive space where all are seen, respected, and accepted.

### Fan Your Flame
www.fan-your-flame.com

Diana Greshtchuk

Fan Your Flame will help you build your financial literacy so you can achieve your dreams and live your best life — for yourself and for generations to come.

### Our Brain Trust
www.ourbraintrust.org

Sherry Deutschmann

BrainTrust is a membership organization for women business owners dedicated to ensuring they have an equal opportunity to build financial independence, wealth, and influence.

### The Quinn Essentials
www.thequinnessentials.com

Andrea Quinn

The Quinn Essentials are nine transformational tools to empower you to create and manifest the life you want to live offered in a live 2-day weekend workshop.

### She Angel Investors
www.sheangelinvestors.com

Catherine Gray

The She Angels mission is to connect female founders and funders to resources and to each other through events, films, podcasts and educational resources.

## BOOKS

*Apparently There Were Complaints by Sharon Gless*

Emmy Award–winning actress Sharon Gless tells all in this laugh-out-loud, juicy, "unforgettably memorable" (Lily Tomlin) memoir about her five decades in Hollywood, where she took on some of the most groundbreaking roles of her time.

*Do Good While Doing Well: Invest for Change, Reap Financial Rewards, and Increase Your Happiness by Marcia Dawood*

Unleash your impact potential with Do Good While Doing Well, a groundbreaking guide designed for those who are eager to make a lasting, meaningful difference, but are unsure how to start. While conventional wisdom may have you believe that charity is the primary, or even only, means for effecting change, this book expands on that notion by introducing you to angel investing as an additional transformative power.

*Learn Lead Lift by Wendy Ryan*

Learn Lead Lift® is the leadership book you'll pick up and return to time and time again. In this easy-to-read and actionable how-to guide, you'll access timely insights cultivated from leaders representing a wide range of identities, backgrounds, roles and industries.

*Love Your Team by Helen Fanucci*

Love Your Team is a conversation-by-conversation survival guide for sales managers who want to thrive in a world where their top talent can walk out the door without taking a single step.

*Lunch with Lucy: Maximize Profits by Investing in Your People by Sherry Stewart Deutschmann*

In this instructional memoir, Deutschmann shares her journey from being a single mother with only a high school education to founding LetterLogic, a $40-million company. Central to her leadership approach was an employee-centric practice she called "Lunch with Lucy," where she would have lunch with any employee who invited her, fostering open communication and empathy within the organization.

*Pitch The Bitch By Kelly Ann Winget*

Pitch the Bitch walks through the female experience in the investment world, on both sides of the financial transaction.

*The Quinn Essentials: 9 Transformational Tools to Accomplish Anything by Andrea Quinn*

These 9 transformational tools will ignite, balance, create or recreate your life whether it's in love relationships, career or your personal life.

*The Startup Investor Mindset: A Guide to Discovering the Top Ways to Influence, Catalyze Innovation, and Impact Early-Stage Ventures as an Investor by Dr. Silvia Mah*

Becoming a great startup investor takes dedication, an abundance mindset, curiosity, engagement, rigor, and empathy. The journey is overflowing with passion and purpose in an uncertain landscape. This guide will empower aspiring investors and experienced investors to better navigate the long trajectory of startup investing.

*Thinking Bigger: A Pitch-Deck Formula for Women Who Want to Change the World by Sarah Dusek*

A guide for women entrepreneurs to help them get the financing they need to build big businesses and change our world.

# PODCASTS

### The Angel Next Door

The Angel Next Door podcast is a show about how people got started investing in startup companies. Hosted by Marcia Dawood, member of the SEC Small Business Capital Formation Advisory Committee and Chair Emeritus of the board of the Angel Capital Association.

### Get Carried Away

A female forward podcast featuring advice from today's business thought leaders and innovators. Host Carrie Murray is the founder of The BRA Network - Business Relationship Alliance, a network of powerful women devoted to advancing female-owned businesses by providing the community, collaboration, mentorship, empowerment and support needed to flourish as an entrepreneur.

### Invest In Her

Invest In Her podcast, hosted by founder of She Angel Investors, Catherine Gray, features phenomenal female founders and funders. The podcast is part of a multimedia platform to connect women with funding resources.

### The Wealth Alpha

The Wealth Alpha Podcast, hosted by entrepreneur, author, founder, public speaker, and alternative investments expert Kelly Ann Winget, is a show about all things money from the seat she dragged to the table.

## COURSES TO EMPOWER YOU

### The Institute for Entrepreneurial Leadership (IFEL)

The Institute for Entrepreneurial Leadership is on a mission to eradicate systemic barriers to capital access. IFEL programs create connections between people whose paths would not ordinarily cross to unlock relationship-based capital for more entrepreneurs and open new opportunities for investors.

### Investing 101 from Fan Your Flame

A comprehensive introductory course designed to equip participants with essential investment knowledge. This course covers key topics such as asset types, title holding, accredited and qualified investor status, investment research and selection, and various investment methods. Participants will also gain insight into essential legal documents, tax planning considerations, and strategies for determining their investment budget. Whether you're new to investing or looking to refine your approach, this course provides the foundational tools to make informed financial decisions.

### The Quinn Essentials

The Quinn Essentials are 9 transformational tools to empower you to create and manifest the life you want to live, offered in a live 2-day weekend workshop.

### 6 Ways to Fund Your Business: Funding Made Simple for Female Founders

This 6 Ways to Fund Your Business course is designed to inform, educate and activate, with the intention of seeing the percentage of women getting funded and witnessing female founders thrive.

### SoGal Foundation

SoGal Foundation's mission is to close the global gender and diversity gap in entrepreneurship and investing by providing accessible and holistic educational resources, including venture capital insights, founder wellness support and tips to help you scale your next billion dollar idea.

All these resources, movie screenings, and more can be found at www.ShowHerTheMoneyMovie.com

**THE END**